The Visions of Revelation

THE GLORY AND MAJESTY OF CHRIST

An Exposition of Revelation 1-22

DENNIS J. PRUTOW

WEM

Westminster Evangelistic Ministries
Pittsburgh, PA

ISBN Paperback 978-0-9885215-5-1

ISBN eBook 978-0-9885215-6-8

Library of Congress Control Number: 2014937304

Printed in the United States of America
at McNaughton & Gunn, Inc., Michigan

Cover Art: Nicora Gangi
Cover Design: Eileen Bechtold

Table of Contents

Revelation: An Introduction

Part One

We begin at the beginning, with an introduction to this great book of exhortations, prophecy, visions, and symbols. I am not interested in debating the various views concerning date, authorship, interpretation, etc. I simply give you my position with some support. I do this so you will understand my approach to Revelation.

First, we take the traditional view that John, the son of Zebedee, the disciple of Jesus and the apostle, wrote Revelation. This is the majority report regarding authorship.

Second, there are two primary views concerning the time of writing. The early date places John's work prior to 70 A.D. and the destruction of Jerusalem. The late date places John's writing at the end of the First Century about 96 A.D. Contemporary advocates of an early date are Jay Adams and Kenneth Gentry. Adams is an amillennialist. Gentry is a postmillennialist. Irenaeus testifies to the late date of Revelation. This is significant since Irenaeus was a student of Polycarp, Bishop of Smyrna, one of the seven churches of Revelation. And Polycarp was, in his youth, a disciple of the apostle John. At this point I personally favor the later date for the book.

Third, I see one of the primary themes of the book of Revelation to be the majesty of Christ. We have before us a divine drama. The Triune God is the main character. Jesus Christ takes center stage and is the One worthy to unfold history. Christ speaks to the church and lays before her consummate blessing and victory. Because the judgments are God's judgments and the victory is God's victory, we ought to come away from Revelation with a deeper appreciation for the greatness, majesty, and glory of Christ.

Fourth, we need to realize, as we study the book of Revelation, that John presents us with many and varied visions. These visions are pictures of reality, not reality itself. Albertus Pieters likens the visions of Revelation to political cartoons. He does not do this to be irreverent. Rather, Pieters wants to make a valid point. Pieters then displays a cartoon from a 1928 edition of the New York *Herald Tribune*.[1] An elephant wraps its trunk around a tiger's tail and joyously swings the tiger overhead.

---

[1] Albertus Pieters, *The Lamb, The Woman and the Dragon* (Grand Rapids, Zondervan, 1937), opposite 36.

THE END OF THE TIGER HUNT
—Darling in the New York *Herald Tribune.*

Currently we do not grasp the meaning. We do not know the historical context. We do not know the symbolism of the tiger. The tiger represents "Tammany Hall, the Democratic organization in New York City."[2] The cartoon portrays the "victory won by the Republican Party in the national election of 1928, when Herbert Hoover was elected president."[3] Pieters says, "We are in a very similar situation with respect to the interpretation of the book of Revelation."[4]

Keeping this in mind, we must be careful to remember Revelation does give us great word pictures. Again, I say, the pictures are not reality itself. They symbolize certain realities. Because Revelation is rich in Hebrew thought, the Old Testament helps us understand many of these symbols. Christ Himself also interprets some of the symbols for us. We ought to humbly allow Scripture to interpret Scripture.

Fifth, there are also several differing approaches to the overall interpretation of Revelation. The Historical interpretation sees Revelation as a record of the history of the church from the time of Christ to the end.

Another view holds that all of Revelation from chapter four forward is future. Fulfillment comes immediately before the Second Advent of Christ. These futurist interpreters fall into two basic categories. The more moderate futurists are classic premillennialists exemplified by George Ladd and Leon

---

[2] Ibid., 38.
[3] Ibid.
[4] Ibid., 38-39.

Morris. The more radical futurists are the dispensationalists. Dispensationalism was popularized in the Schofield Reference Bible.

The preterist interpretation sees almost the entire book of Revelation as fulfilled in the first two or three centuries of the Christian era. Preterist means past. The preterist is also more likely to be postmillennial in approach and to argue for the early date for Revelation.

Another school of thought looks at Revelation as a "philosophy of history." James Ramsey represents this school of thought. He says Revelation

> was not intended to give beforehand a history of particular events, but to present the principles that were to shape the world's history, so far as it concerned the progress of the divine kingdom, in their chief combinations and workings, and so to unfold the general course and grand characteristics of God's dealings with His church and the nations during the long ages of conflict and darkness through which the church was to pass,—the various forms and combinations of evil that should oppose her, and the power by which she should overcome, and the glory that should eventually crown her triumph.[5]

Part Two

I am partial to this "philosophy of history" approach to Revelation. I also agree with Henry Barclay Swete who says of his exposition of Revelation:

> With the 'preterists' it will take its stand on the circumstances of the age and the locality to which the book belongs . . . ; with the 'futurists' it will look for the fulfillments of St. John's pregnant words in times yet to come. With the school of Auberlin and Benson it will find in the Apocalypse a Christian philosophy of history; with the 'continuous-historical' school it can see in the progress of events ever-new illustrations of the working of the great principles, which are revealed.[6]

No approach to Revelation has a monopoly on the truth. Each has its drawbacks.

Sixth, I hold that this wonderful book of Revelation is divided into seven parallel sections recapitulating, from different perspectives, the time between the first and second advents. As Murray begins a brief exposition of Jesus' discourse on the Mount of Olives, he notes Matthew 24:4-14 gives "a forecast of interadventual history," a brief outline of the period between the first coming of Christ and the second.[7] Murray then notes:

> Verses 15-28 comprise another section of the discourse. This section is not a continuation, because verse 14 had brought us up to the end. It must be, to

---

[5] James B. Ramsey, *The Book of Revelation: An Exposition of the First Eleven Chapters* (Carlisle, PA: The Banner of Truth Trust, 1977), 35.

[6] Henry B. Swete, *Commentary on Revelation* (Grand Rapids: Kregel Publications, 1977), ccviii.

[7] John Murray, *Collected Writings of John Murray, 4 vols.* (Carlisle, PA: The Banner of Truth Trust, 1976-82), 2:388.

some extent, recapitulation. Our Lord forecasts to the disciples certain additional features that had been delineated in verses 4-14, and gives the warnings and exhortations appropriate to the events involved. *Here we have a principle, which must be applied in the interpretation of prophecy.* Delineation of the eschatological drama is not always continuously progressive; it is often recapitulatory. But recapitulation is not repetition (italics mine).[8]

Milton Terry suggests, "John's Apocalypse is but an enlargement of our Lord's eschatological discourse on the Mount of Olives."[9] If Murray and Terry are right, Revelation will use parallel sections and recapitulation. Geoffrey Wilson says, "The dominant place which is given to the number seven has convinced some scholars that the book consists of seven parallel sections, each which depicts the church's conflict throughout the gospel age from a different standpoint."[10] Wilson's outline follows:

Section 1: *Christ among the seven churches* (chs 1-3).
    The seven letters speak to the church in every age, because they show that the glorified Christ is always with his people, both in judgment to call them to repentance and in grace to assure them of victory.

Section 2: *The Lamb and the seven seals* (chs 4 -7).
    The vision of heaven reveals the victorious Lamb as the only one who is worthy to take the book with seven seals. These he opens one by one, thus securing the judgment of the wicked and the bliss of the redeemed.

Section *3: The seven trumpets of judgment* (chs 8 -11).
    The first six warning judgments fail to bring the wicked to repentance and, though the witnessing church must suffer persecution, all these wrongs are avenged when the seventh trumpet heralds the final judgment.

Section 4: *The woman and the dragon* (chs 12-14).
    As the woman gives birth to a son, the dragon (Satan) waits to devour him, but the child is caught up to heaven. The dragon now persecutes the woman and is assisted by the beast from the sea and the beast from the earth. The section ends with a vision of Christ's coming in judgment.

Section 5: *The seven bowls of wrath* (chs 15, *16).*
    In this vision there is portrayed the outpouring of God's wrath upon the impenitent and the terror of the last judgment.

Section *6: The fall of Babylon* (chs 17-19).
    The fall of the godless city is followed by rejoicing in heaven, and the destruction of the beast and the false prophet is depicted in a further account of Christ's second coming.

---

[8] Ibid.
[9] Milton S. Terry, *Biblical Apocalyptics* (Grand Rapids: Baker Book House, 1988), 269.
[10] Geoffrey B. Wilson, *Revelation* (Welwyn, England: Evangelical Press, 1985), 11.

Section 7: *Christ's victory over Satan* (chs 20 -22).

During the gospel age Satan is bound so that he may no longer deceive the nations, but he is released for the last battle, only to be overthrown at Christ's return, when the present universe is replaced by the new heaven and the new earth.[11]

There is another similarity with Matthew 24-25. Matthew 24:3 records, "As He [Jesus] was sitting on the Mount of Olives, the disciples came to Him privately, saying, 'Tell us, when will these things happen, and what will be the sign of Your coming, and of the end of the age?'" This question comes immediately after Jesus predicts doom for the temple. In response, the disciples ask their threefold question. The question and the answer span the interval between Jesus' first coming and the second. Note there is more emphasis upon the destruction of the temple early in Matthew 24 while the emphasis falls upon final judgment as we move on to Matthew 25.

In a similar way, the first section of Revelation gives us letters to existent churches. The final section of Revelation emphasizes the final state of believers with God in glory. As we move through the seven sections of the book, emphasis shifts to the final glorious victory of God over evil and the participation of the saints in that victory.

One final word of introduction is needed. Some will ask what commentaries I have found particularly useful and helpful. Check the notes. I find three commentaries particularly helpful. They are Albertus Pieters, *The Lamb, The Woman and the Dragon*; James Ramsey, *Revelation*; and Geoffrey Wilson, *Revelation*.[12]

---

[11] Ibid., 11-12.

[12] See also my suggestions on page 75.

Revelation: Prologue and Salutation

Revelation 1:1-8

We begin the exposition proper with the prologue, Revelation 1:1-3:

> The Revelation of Jesus Christ, which God gave Him to show to His bond-servants, the things which must soon take place; and He sent and communicated it by His angel to His bond-servant, John, who testified to the word of God and to the testimony of Jesus Christ, even to all that he saw. Blessed is he who reads and those who hear the words of the prophecy, and heed the things, which are written in it for the time is near.

The book before us is an unveiling given to us by Jesus Christ. Although it includes a revelation of Christ Himself, it is not primarily an unveiling of Christ. This is the case since the revelation comes from God the Father and is given to Christ. In turn, Our Lord gives this revelation to His servants.

The revelation given by God to His Son and passed to the servants of Christ involves the things which must shortly take place. Beyond doubt, the book is written to early Christians and is meant to undergird their faith regarding impending Providences of God. Although we may place emphasis on impending events, the text also places emphasis on the *necessity* of these events. Jesus tells the disciples concerning their own time and the events surrounding the collapse of the Jewish nation, "All these things are merely the beginning of birth pangs" (Matthew 24:8). More will follow.

The revelation comes from God to Christ then to John by the mediation of Christ's angel. Angels play a large role in Revelation. They are messengers, which transmit and carry out the purposes of God. The similarity is with Moses who received the law at Sinai through the mediation of angels (Acts 7:53, Galatians 3:19, Hebrews 2:2).

John then bore witness, through his book, to the word of God and the testimony of Jesus. He did so by setting forth all that he saw in writing so we can all benefit from the revelation.

As a result, there is great blessing attached to those who read, hear, and take heed to the book containing these visions. Verse 3 is the first of *seven* beatitudes in the book of Revelation. It carries the same form as those uttered by Jesus in Matthew 5:1-9. Reference is to the *public reading* of Revelation. The assembly of God's people is the temple of the Holy Spirit. It is a unique place for reading God's word and for the application of that word to the hearts of men and women. When you heed this book, you grasp the majesty and glory of Christ. You live under the power of His majesty. "The conclusion, when all has been heard, is: fear God and keep His commandments" (Ecclesiastes 12:13). The study of Revelation is therefore not simply brain candy.

Verses 4-6 give the salutation:

John to the seven churches that are in Asia: Grace to you and peace, from Him who is and who was and who is to come, and from the seven Spirits who are before His throne, and from Jesus Christ, the faithful witness, the firstborn of the dead, and the ruler of the kings of the earth. To Him who loves us and released us from our sins by His blood and has made us to be a kingdom, priests to His God and Father; to Him be the glory and the dominion forever and ever. Amen.

John faithfully transmits the visions received to real people in real time. Although this is the case, the number seven refers to perfection, completeness and fullness. The seven churches are representative. We acknowledge this is the case when we read the apostle Paul. He also wrote to seven churches, the churches at Rome, Corinth, Galatia, Ephesus, Philippi, Colossae, and Thessalonica. We accept these letters as directed to specific people but also directed to the church at large throughout history. In like manner, the letters to the seven churches of Revelation are also to us.

We now hear the gospel. Grace to you. Grace comes in the form of the work of Christ and the Holy Spirit enabling men and women to embrace Christ. There is then peace with God. "Therefore having been justified by faith, we have peace with God through our Lord Jesus Christ through whom also we have obtained our introduction by faith into this grace in which we stand" (Romans 5:1-2).

This grace comes from the Father who is eternal, the beginning and the end. He is the fountain of grace. "Blessed be the God and Father of our Lord Jesus Christ who has blessed us with every spiritual blessing" (Ephesians 1:3). The Holy Spirit mediates this grace and peace. The number seven indicates He is a perfect, all wise, all-powerful, all gracious Spirit.

Finally, this grace and peace come to us on the basis of the work of Jesus Christ. He is the faithful witness to the plans and purposes of God. He was crucified, dead, and buried. He rose again the third day. He is the firstborn of God worthy to receive all of heaven and earth as an inheritance. He therefore sits on the throne of heaven as Lord of all.

This Jesus demonstrates the love of God in His death and resurrection on behalf of sinners. He thereby releases men and women from the ruling power of sin. He forms His people into a new kingdom. They are priests who offer sacrifices of praise to God because this God is indeed the source and wellspring of all grace and peace. The salutation properly ends with doxology.

John adds to this doxology a word concerning the coming of Christ. "Behold, He is coming with the clouds, and every eye will see Him, even those who pierced Him; and all the tribes of the earth will mourn over Him. So it is to be. Amen" (Revelation 1:7). We begin to get a flavor of the symbolism involved in the book with these words. Christ will come a second time in glory. Those who pierced Him, those guilty of sins making it necessary for Him to die, will see Him. Citizens of heaven, Christians, will rejoice at their salvation. The tribes of the earth, unbelievers, will mourn their judgment before the King.

This opening section of Revelation concludes with triumphant words of the Father, "'I am the Alpha and the Omega,' says the Lord God, 'who is and who was and who is to come, the Almighty'" (Revelation 1:8). God is the eternal One. We must know His eternal majesty, His mighty power, His blessed holiness, justice, grace, mercy, and love. And we will.

The Vision of Christ

Revelation 1:9-20

Revelation 1:9-11, introduces the great vision of the Master, Jesus Christ:

> I, John, your brother and fellow partaker in the tribulation and kingdom and perseverance which are in Jesus, was on the island called Patmos because of the word of God and the testimony of Jesus. I was in the Spirit on the Lord's day, and I heard behind me a loud voice like the sound of a trumpet, saying, "Write in a book what you see, and send it to the seven churches: to Ephesus and to Smyrna and to Pergamum and to Thyatira and to Sardis and to Philadelphia and to Laodicea."

John is a brother to all the Christians in Asia Minor and a fellow member of Christ's kingdom. He is a participant in their tribulation. He preaches perseverance and lives patiently before God. This patience and perseverance result from union and communion with Christ.

Traditionally, John was banished to Patmos, "a small rocky island in the Aegean Sea lying about thirty-seven miles west-southwest of Miletus . . ."[13] (See Acts 20:17). John was exiled to Patmos "because" of his testimony that Christ is Lord of all and "because" he preached this doctrine. "Committal to an island was a device used by provincial governors to rid themselves of men of high rank whose influence upon others was deemed to be harmful."[14]

John was taken up in a state of ecstasy and rapture. He passed the barrier separating this life with the spiritual realm. God thus transported him on the Lord's Day. The word translated *Lord's* is an adjective used in only one other place in the New Testament. In 1 Corinthians 11:20, Paul uses the word to designate the Lord's Supper. This is the Supper and the Day uniquely belonging to the Lord. The Lord's Day is the first day of the week, resurrection day. It is the day memorializing God's redemption (Deuteronomy 5:15).

John heard a voice like a trumpet. The trumpet call is a warning, a call to gather God's people, or a summons to action. Israel responded to the trumpet call to invade and crush Jericho. The significance of the message John is about to hear is accentuated by the trumpet-sounding voice. The voice commands John to put the visions into writing and deliver his book to all the churches.

John naturally turns to see who is speaking to him. Verse 12: "Then I turned to see the voice that was speaking with me. And having turned I saw seven golden lampstands." John sees seven golden candelabra. These are lampstands similar to the one found in the tabernacle. Each had seven lamps. "The seven lampstands are the seven churches" (Revelation 1:20). The church is to shed perfect light in a dark and sinful world (Matthew 5:14). The oil for the lamps comes from God (Compare Zechariah 4).

---

[13] Wilson, 20.
[14] Ibid., 21.

Verse 13: "And in the middle of the lampstands I saw one like the Son of Man, clothed in a robe reaching to the feet, and girded across His chest with a golden sash." Christ walks in the midst of His church, in the midst of His people. The title, Son of Man, emphasizes Christ's deity (Daniel 7:13). He is robed as the high priest of God and carries the ephod on His breast over His heart.

Again, we must realize the church of Christ is a special dwelling place of God in the Spirit (Ephesians 2:22). "You also, as living stones, are being built up as a spiritual house for a holy priesthood, to offer up spiritual sacrifices acceptable to God through Jesus Christ" (1 Peter 2:5).

God is essentially present everywhere (Psalm 139:7). God is graciously present in heaven and present in wrath in hell (Psalm 139:8). God's presence in the Old Testament temple differed from His general presence with the people of God. Similarly, Christ's gracious presence with His gathered people differs significantly from His general presence in the world. Christ is present with His church with special grace to apply His word to human hearts and change lives.

John now proceeds with a description of Christ. Verse 14: "His head and His hair were white like white wool, like snow; and His eyes were like a flame of fire." Christ is shown with a white head of wisdom (Proverbs 16:31). His eyes are burning, penetrating, and piercing. "The eyes of the Lord are in every place, watching the evil and the good" (Proverbs 15:3).

Verse 15: "His feet were like burnished bronze, when it has been made to glow in a furnace, and His voice was like the sound of many waters." Christ does not have feet of clay like the feet of the image in Daniel 2:34 which were destroyed by God's kingdom. He strides through history with strength. His voice is one of power. Anyone who stands by Niagara Falls and hears the power of that water can understand this symbol.

Verse 16: "In His right hand He held seven stars, and out of His mouth came a sharp two-edged sword; and His face was like the sun shining in its strength." "The seven stars are the angels of the seven churches" (Revelation 1:20). Angels are messengers (Matthew 11:10). The primary messengers in the churches are the pastors. Christ has them in His hand. What comfort and care. Christ also speaks the word of God in grace and in judgment (Hebrews 4:12).

John's reaction is simple:

> I fell at His feet like a dead man. And He placed His right hand on me, saying, "Do not be afraid; I am the first and the last, and the living One; and I was dead, and behold, I am alive forevermore, and I have the keys of death and of Hades. Therefore write the things which you have seen, and the things which are, and the things which will take place after these things" (Revelation 1:17-19).

It is as though the wind is knocked out of John and his heart stops. He falls on His face before Christ. He then hears wonderful words, "Do not fear." The disciples heard these words on the Sea of Galilee (Mark 6:50, Luke 5:10) and on the mount of transfiguration (Matthew 17:7). Christ then speaks of Himself as equal with God. He is the first and the last. Compare Revelation 1:8. Christ is back from the dead. He is the one who has the keys of death and hell. That is, Christ has authority over life and death. "Do not fear those who kill the body but are unable to kill the soul; but rather fear Him who is able to destroy both soul and body in hell" (Matthew 10:28). We must stand in awe of the majesty of Christ.

The Seven Churches

Revelation 2-3

As we begin a look at the seven letters to the seven churches, we take note of the universal application of these letters to the church at large through all ages. The Spirit sets the stage in this regard. Revelation 2:1-2, "To the angel of the church in Ephesus write: The One who holds the seven stars in His right hand, the One who walks among the seven golden lampstands, says this."

THE PROVINCE OF ASIA (Western part)

There is little doubt this letter is directed to a particular church, Ephesus. This city was a prominent seaport in Asia Minor. (See map above).[15] It was a large city, some 250,000. It was the home of the world famous cult of Diana. Acts 19:24, "For a man named Demetrius, a silversmith, who made silver shrines of Artemis, was bringing no little business to the craftsmen." This false worship

---

[15] Geoffrey B Wilson, *Revelation* (Welwyn, England: Evangelical Press, 1985), 8.

brought great economic gain to many and the citizens of this city were generally quite affluent.

The introduction of the gospel was an immediate threat to the economy. Acts 19:27, "Not only is there danger that this trade of ours fall into disrepute, but also that the temple of the great goddess, Artemis, be regarded as worthless and that she whom all of Asia and the world worship will even be dethroned from her magnificence." For this reason, if for no other, tradesmen opposed the gospel. The results of affluence seemed to penetrate the church also.

But was this particular letter directed only to Ephesus? I do not think so for several reasons. First, there are *seven* letters. Christ holds the *seven* stars. He walks among the *seven* lampstands.

The number seven refers to completeness or perfection. We have in these seven letters a complete rehearsal of the difficulties faced within the church of Jesus Christ. As mentioned, it is of no small consequence that we also have letters written by the apostle Paul directed to *seven* different churches. We have letters to the church at Rome, Corinth, Galatia, Ephesus, Philippi, Colossae and Thessalonica. We rightly take these letters written to specific churches as given to the church at large. So too, were the letters to the seven churches of Revelation 2 and 3.

Second, Christ describes Himself as, "The One who holds the seven stars in His right hand, the One who walks among the seven golden lampstands." We have already seen the interpretation. Jesus says, "As for the mystery of the seven stars which you saw in My right hand, and the seven golden lampstands: the seven stars are the angels of the seven churches, and the seven lampstands are the seven churches" (Revelation 1:20).

The angels are messengers. The primary messenger in the church is the pastor. He communicates the message sent from God. Christ holds the pastors of His church in His hand. If the number seven represents completeness, Christ holds the complete ministry of the church in His hand.

Christ walks among His churches and walks within His churches. The lampstands are candelabra like the one designed by God for use in the tabernacle so that each contains *seven* lights. "Six branches shall go out from its sides; three branches of the lampstand from its one side and three branches of the lampstand from its other side" (Exodus 25:32). The church of Christ must be aglow with the perfect light of God.

Jesus made a startling statement to His disciples. "While I am in the world, I am the Light of the world" (John 9:5). *While I am in the world*, said Jesus. He then described the work of the church saying, "You are the light of the world" (Matthew 5:14). Christ walks among the lampstands in order to provide them light to shine in this sin-darkened world.

So a lesson here is that Christ calls His church to take His light into the darkness. From this perspective, the letters to the seven churches reveal various ways the light of Christ may be dimmed or may shine more brightly.

Finally, each of the seven letters ends with this comment from Christ. "He who has an ear, let him hear what the Spirit says to the churches" (Revelation

2:7). Each letter ends with an exhortation for each church to listen to and hear what the Spirit is saying to all the churches. These letters are not designed for one but for all. We look at them to discern lessons for the church at large and for our individual congregations. There are lessons in each letter for each of our own congregations. May God give us grace to see, hear, and understand.

One final word regarding the seven letters. We must understand as we gather for worship that Jesus Christ upholds the ministry of the church, which faithfully reflects His light, maintains the standards of His word, carefully and forcefully proclaims that word, and seeks to follow Christ by the power of the Spirit.

As we gather for worship in faithfulness to Christ, the Lord Himself walks in our midst. We do not see Him with our physical eyes or hear Him move among us. Yet Christ is present by the power of His Spirit to change our lives and conform us to His image. He is present to speak through His word. He is present as the morning star to arise in our hearts.

The Letter to Ephesus

Revelation 2:1-7

After the To and From lines in each letter, Christ makes a statement concerning His knowledge of the church. This is a statement of commendation and/or condemnation. Here Christ commends the Ephesians: "I know your deeds and your toil and perseverance, and that you cannot tolerate evil men, and you put to the test those who call themselves apostles, and they are not, and you found them to be false" (Revelation 2:2).

Christ's knowledge is not simply special understanding derived from an ability to see into our hearts. The knowledge Christ speaks of is open to view. It is knowledge based upon sight. It is not hidden special knowledge.

"I know your deeds and your toil and perseverance." Here is a church known because of her deeds. She is a picture of James 1:25, "One who looks intently at the perfect law, the law of liberty, and abides by it, not having become a forgetful hearer but an effectual doer, this man will be blessed in what he does." The doing of the word of God often entails toil, very hard work. We are not permitted to coast in the Christian life. Jesus put it this way, "We must work the works of Him who sent Me as long as it is day; night is coming when no one can work" (John 9:4).

Christians must also persevere in the work God has given them in this life. I think one of the most important qualities of a pastor or missionary is perseverance. The pastor must continue on in his work through thick and thin, through all the ups and downs. There are difficult times and there are rewards. We remember the call of Isaiah and Isaiah's response. "Then I heard the voice of the Lord, saying, 'Whom shall I send, and who will go for Us?' Then I said, 'Here am I. Send me!'" (Isaiah 6:8). We fail to look at the commission God gave Isaiah. Perseverance is required to follow the assignment given by God.

> He said, "Go, and tell this people: 'Keep on listening, but do not perceive; keep on looking, but do not understand.' Render the hearts of this people insensitive, their ears dull, and their eyes dim, otherwise they might see with their eyes, hear with their ears, understand with their hearts, and return and be healed" (Isaiah 6:9-10).

Those outside the church can observe this perseverance.

Christ emphasizes the importance of perseverance in verse 3. "And you have perseverance and have endured for My name's sake, and have not grown weary." This is a stick-to-it attitude of heart based upon a desire to see the name of Christ exalted and lifted up. This is not a self-centered persistence based upon self-exaltation. "Come, let us build for ourselves a city, and a tower whose top will reach into heaven, and let us make for ourselves a name, otherwise we will be scattered abroad over the face of the whole earth" (Genesis 11:4).

The church must test those teachers who come along to see if they are indeed sent by God. We must reject those who claim authority from God but fail

20

to follow the word of God. We must detect false teaching and reject it. But it is not just the false teaching that is the problem. We must detect false teachers and insure the church does not embrace them in her ministry. God commended Ephesus for this. Will He commend us in like manner?

In each letter except two, Christ has a word of rebuke. Only two of the seven letters contain no word of warning or censure. In other words, only a minority of the church stands in a position of receiving only commendation. Most churches stand in need of correction. We should be honest in our self-evaluation at this point.

Verse 4: "But I have this against you, that you have left your first love." This is a most devastating critique. All manner of activity can be technically correct without proper motives. "If I have the gift of prophecy, and know all mysteries and all knowledge; and if I have all faith, so as to remove mountains, but do not have love, I am nothing. And if I give all my possessions to feed the poor, and if I surrender my body to be burned, but do not have love, it profits me nothing" (1 Corinthians 13:2-3). Love, as fully described in Scripture, is the normative sign of the presence of the Holy Spirit in a human life. This church has left its first love.

The devotion of heart once experienced after conversion has waned. This is not normal. John the baptizer "was the lamp that was burning and was shining and you were willing to rejoice for a while in his light" (John 5:35). We too must be lamps having heat as well as light. We must have affections burning for Christ. Lamps with low flames because of little oil are unacceptable.

Verse 5: "Therefore remember from where you have fallen, and repent and do the deeds you did at first; or else I am coming to you and will remove your lampstand out of its place unless you repent." A change of heart is needed. Remember your former state when you had deep joy and exaltation in Christ.

You have fallen. The idea here is that of falling from a proper understanding of grace. There is reliance upon self-righteousness as obtaining merit before God. It is the idea of Galatians 5:4, "You have been severed from Christ, you who are seeking to be justified by law; you have fallen from grace."

Verse 6: "Yet this you do have, that you hate the deeds of the Nicolaitans, which I also hate." We know nothing of the Nicolaitans except that they were opposed to the Law of God. They were antinomian. The Ephesians were not antinomian. They too hated that devilish doctrine. But perhaps they lapsed into a Pharisaical tendency by leaning too much upon their own merit. Love was lost. Legalism was the problem.

Verse 7: "He who has an ear, let him hear what the Spirit says to the churches. To him who overcomes, I will grant to eat of the tree of life which is in the Paradise of God." We need to listen to the rebuke. "For this reason I remind you to kindle afresh the gift of God" (2 Timothy 1:6). The rekindling process begins with understanding the problem and seeking the face of God for needed grace and renewal. There is a reward. It is access to the tree of life in the garden of God. Are we listening?

The Letter to Smyrna

Revelation 2:8-11

Revelation 2:8: "And to the angel of the church in Smyrna write: The first and the last, who was dead, and has come to life, says this."

> Smyrna, the only one of the seven cities still in existence (modern Izmir), lays some thirty-five miles north of Ephesus. This beautiful city and prosperous port (c. 200,000 pop.), claiming to be the first city in Asia and a faithful ally of Rome, was in fact the first province to build a temple to the goddess Roma in 195 B.C. Its large colony of Jews used their influence with the authorities to persecute Christians, and later assisted in the martyrdom of the aged Polycarp (A.D. 156). The faithful church in Smyrna receives the shortest letter and the warmest praise.[16]

Verse 2:9: "I know your tribulation and your poverty (but you are rich), and the blasphemy by those who say they are Jews and are not, but are a synagogue of Satan." Christ says to this church that He knows their earthly poverty. This poverty was visible. At the same time, these people were rich in Christ. They were quite the opposite of the Christians in Laodicea, as Revelation 3:17-18 indicates:

> Because you say, "I am rich, and have become wealthy, and have need of nothing," and you do not know that you are wretched and miserable and poor and blind and naked, I advise you to buy from Me gold refined by fire so that you may become rich, and white garments so that you may clothe yourself, and that the shame of your nakedness will not be revealed; and eye salve to anoint your eyes so that you may see.

Those outside the pale of the church blasphemed the Christians. They reviled the church and uttered impieties against her. Jews according to the flesh in Smyrna opposed the church and persecuted her. Christ calls the Jewish synagogue, filled with those who despised and rejected Christ as Messiah, the Synagogue of Satan. In our day, worshippers opposed to Christ compose gatherings of the devil. Although these are harsh words, they come from Christ.

Christ now offers words of comfort, warning and consolation. Verse 10: "Do not fear what you are about to suffer. Behold, the devil is about to cast some of you into prison, so that you will be tested, and you will have tribulation for ten days. Be faithful until death, and I will give you the crown of life."

Polycarp, Bishop of Smyrna, bore witness to the type of suffering faced by the church. He also gave testimony to the lack of fear exhorted by Christ. James Ramsey comments:

---

[16] Geoffrey B. Wilson, *Revelation* (Welwyn, England: Evangelical Press, 1985), 31.

Polycarp, its chief bishop and a disciple of the apostle John, suffered martyrdom here in extreme old age. The narrative has been often repeated, but we cannot refrain from giving here at least the answers of the aged martyr when summoned before the proconsul, and addressed in the customary language— "Swear, curse Christ, and I will set you free." "Eighty and six years have I served Him; I have received only good at His hands. Can I then curse Him, my King and my Savior?" "I will cast you to the wild beasts if you do not change your mind," said the proconsul. "Bring the wild beasts thither," said Polycarp, "for change my mind from the better to the worse I will not." "Do you despise the wild beasts? I will subdue your spirit by the flames." "The flames which you menace endure but for the time, and are soon extinguished." Calmly rejoined the martyr; "but there is a fire reserved for the wicked, whereof you know not; the fire of a judgment to come, and of punishment everlasting." These flames soon did their work. By his death, the rage of the populace, to which already many victims had been sacrificed, was so far satiated that the proconsul suspended the persecution, and this poor suffering church had a respite.[17]

The persecution, says Christ, is a work of the devil. We will see this clearly in Revelation 12. It reminds us of Job. The persecution itself is prison if it is not literal imprisonment. God locks us in persecution for testing. As Paul boldly says in Romans 5:3-4, "And not only this, but we also exult in our tribulations, knowing that tribulation brings about perseverance; and perseverance, proven character; and proven character, hope." Tribulation, testing, has a way of proving the quality of Christian character. Sometimes the tests are severe.

Christ says the period of testing will be relatively short, ten days. Ten refers to completion and perfection from a human perspective. The time of testing will be correct to prove the character of the Christians at Smyrna before a watching world. Polycarp is an example.

Christians must be faithful until death. Jesus reminds us, "In the world you have tribulation, but take courage; I have overcome the world" (John 16:33). Paul declares, "Through many tribulations we must enter the kingdom of God" (Acts 14:22). We may retire from our various vocations at age 65 but there is no retirement in the Christian faith.

The crown of life awaits those who persevere in faith and love. The crown is the reward of the athlete. You must run the race fully and faithfully. The Christian's crown is the reward of eternal life. "Blessed is a man who perseveres under trial; for once he has been approved, he will receive the crown of life which the Lord has promised to those who love Him" (James 1:12).

Verse 11: "He who has an ear, let him hear what the Spirit says to the churches. He who overcomes will not be hurt by the second death." Physical hearing is one thing. Spiritual hearing is quite another. Spiritual hearing comes as a result of spiritual rebirth. Compare Acts 16:14. Spiritual rebirth is the first

---

[17] James B. Ramsey, *The Book of Revelation, An Exposition of the First Eleven Chapters* (Carlisle, PA: The Banner of Truth Trust, 1977), 135.

23

resurrection (Ephesians 2:5). "Blessed and holy is the one who has a part in the first resurrection; over these the second death has no power" (Revelation 20:6). The second death is the lake of fire (Revelation 20:14).

The Letter to Pergamum

Revelation 2:12-17

We move up the coast of the Aegean Sea fifty to fifty-five miles to a third seaport city, Pergamum, located on the Caicus River a few miles from the sea. Revelation 2:12: "And to the angel of the church in Pergamum write: The One who has the sharp two-edged sword says this."

We note two things about this center of commerce. First, Pergamum, for the time, had an immense library of 200,000 volumes:

> By its devotion to literature, this city has inscribed its name upon the very structure of our own language. The king of Egypt would not permit the exportation of the papyrus plant, which was then used for writing, as we use paper, and from which the word "paper" is derived; and the philosophers of Pergamos were under the necessity of providing a substitute. This they did by preparing sheep skins and goatskins in a peculiar way, and on these they were accustomed to writing their books. The preparation of these skins was brought to perfection in Pergamos, and from this circumstance they were called "Pergamana Charta," a name which has been contracted and modified by passing through various languages until it stands in our tongue, parchment; that is, paper of Pergamos, a name which will forever commemorate the inhabitants of Pergamos in the pursuits of literature.[18]

Second, Pergamum was also a center of idolatry. She had temples to various Greek gods and goddesses. Among the centers of worship was a temple to Aesculapius, the god of medicine and healing. "The popularity of this cult made Pergamum the 'Lourdes' of the ancient world (R. H. Charles)."[19] Pergamum was also the first city "in Asia to erect a temple to Augustus (29 B.C.) . . . "[20] As such it was a center for the imperial cult.

Christ reminds this church He is the One with the sharp two-edged sword. He comes in power to bless His people but He also comes in judgment. The sword is the word of God (Ephesians 6:17). The word brings healing or correction. The former may come through the latter.

Verse 13: "I know where you dwell, where Satan's throne is; and you hold fast My name, and did not deny My faith even in the days of Antipas, My witness, My faithful one, who was killed among you, where Satan dwells." As in the cases of Ephesus and Smyrna, Christ gives a word of commendation to Pergamum. Christ knows the people dwell among much evil. The throne of Satan indicates this city is a capital of evil. The people were required to confess, "Caesar is Lord." The basic Christian confession is, "Christ is Lord" (Romans 10:9). Under pressure, the church maintained its commitment to Christ and did

---

[18] William J. Reid, *Lectures on the Revelation* (Pittsburgh: Stevenson, Foster and Company, 1878), 47.

[19] Geoffrey B. Wilson, *Revelation* (Welwyn, England: Evangelical Press, 1985), 33.

[20] Ibid.

not deny Him. The people remembered the words of Jesus, "Therefore everyone who confesses Me before men, I will also confess him before My Father who is in heaven. But whoever denies Me before men, I will also deny him before My Father who is in heaven" (Matthew 10:32-33).

The Lord mentions a martyr, Antipas. We know nothing else of him. He would have been famous to those of Pergamum as Polycarp is so well remembered for his faithful witness to Christ in Smyrna.

Verse 14: "But I have a few things against you, because you have there some who hold the teaching of Balaam, who kept teaching Balak to put a stumbling block before the sons of Israel, to eat things sacrificed to idols and to commit acts of immorality." Some members of the church might be praiseworthy. But there were problems.

Balaam was a false prophet eager to please men and fill his pockets. When Israel came out of Egypt and approached Moab, Balak, king of Moab, hired Balaam to curse Israel. "So the elders of Moab and the elders of Midian departed with the fees for divination in their hand; and they came to Balaam and repeated Balak's words to him" (Numbers 22:7). Balaam also advised Israel to practice idolatry and sensuousness, as she had done at the foot of Mount Sinai. "Behold, these caused the sons of Israel, through the counsel of Balaam, to trespass against the Lord in the matter of Peor, so the plague was among the congregation of the Lord" (Numbers 31:16).

At Pergamum some were "forsaking the right way." They "followed the way of Balaam, the son of Beor, who loved the wages of unrighteousness" (2 Peter 2:15). "For pay they have rushed headlong into the error of Balaam" (Jude 11). The church was therefore a mixed multitude (Exodus 12:38, Numbers 11:4).

Verse 15: "So you also have some who in the same way hold the teaching of the Nicolaitans." The Nicolaitans were antinomians. They opposed God's law as a standard for Christian living. These Nicolaitans would not halt the course of idolatry but give license to it. This is often the case in our culture. Adultery and fornication, violations of the Seventh Commandment, are not seen as incompatible with a Christian confession.

Verse 16: "Therefore repent; or else I am coming to you quickly, and I will make war against them with the sword of My mouth." The proper answer to idolatry and sensuality is repentance. You must change your mind about these sins and view them as God views them. Failure to do so will result in experiencing the judgmental side of Christ's sword. This may mean judgment in this life. It may mean eternal perdition. Christ will make war against those in the church who reject His ways.

Verse 17: "He who has an ear, let him hear what the Spirit says to the churches. To him who overcomes, to him I will give some of the hidden manna, and I will give him a white stone, and a new name written on the stone which no one knows but he who receives it." We must not casually dismiss the words of the Spirit as though they do not apply to us. Christ is the hidden manna, the bread of heaven, hidden in heaven. Jury verdicts were given by placing a black or white stone in a box. Christ says He will give a white stone to those who overcome. They "shall be openly acknowledged and acquitted in the day of judgment" (WSC, Answer 38).

The Letter to Thyatira

Revelation 2:18-29

Part One

We come to the fourth of the seven churches. Thyatira is southeast of Pergamum about forty miles. The city was known for the roots of a plant from which red dye was manufactured.[21] It was a center of industry, commerce, affluence, trade guilds, and pagan religious practices. We recall Acts 16:14 where Paul went to a riverside in Philippi. "A woman named Lydia, from the city of Thyatira, a seller of purple fabrics, a worshipper of God, was listening; and the Lord opened her heart to respond to the things spoken by Paul." It is possible Lydia took the gospel back to Thyatira.

Revelation 2:18: "And to the angel of the church in Thyatira write: The Son of God, who has eyes like a flame of fire, and His feet are like burnished bronze, says this." We have what I have called a memo. It is addressed *to* the church at Thyatira through her pastor. *Angel* means *messenger*. The chief messenger of God within a congregation is the pastor.

The memo is *from* the Son of God. He is described as the one with penetrating eyes who sees beyond outward appearance. He strides through history with power (Revelation 1:14-15). He does not have feet of clay (Daniel 2:33-34). He brings sure and burning judgment.

In verse 19, Christ commends the church. "I know your deeds, and your love and faith and service and perseverance, and that your deeds of late are greater than at first." The deeds of the church comport with the profession made by this body of believers. This church lives James 2:22, "You see that faith was working with his [their] works, and as a result of the works, faith was perfected." The faith of members of this church was shown *mature* as they exercised "faith working through love" (Galatians 5:7).

This church also embodies James 2:24. "You see that a man is justified by works and not by faith alone." *Justified* is translated *vindicated* in Matthew 11:19, "Wisdom is vindicated by her deeds." The faith of persons professing Christ is *vindicated* by their works. Love, faith and, service are tied together in them.

Growth and sanctification are also taking place among these believers. "Your deeds of late are greater than at first" (verse 19). Such sanctification is essential. "Pursue peace with all men, and the sanctification without which no one will see the Lord" (Hebrews 12:14).

With all this commendation, Christ also indicates His displeasure with Thyatira. "But I have this against you, that you tolerate the woman Jezebel, who calls herself a prophetess, and she teaches and leads My bond-servants astray so that they commit acts of immorality and eat things sacrificed to idols" (verse 20).

---

[21] Reid, 54.

28

While increasing in love, faith, service, and perseverance, Christians ought not to tolerate evil or heresy in the church. The name Jezebel immediately reminds us of the infamous Old Testament character. Concerning Ahab, 1 Kings 16:31 says, "It came about, as though it had been a trivial thing for him to walk in the sins of Jeroboam the son of Nebat, that he married Jezebel the daughter of Ethbaal king of the Sidonians, and went to serve Baal and worshipped him." Jezebel exercised undue influence over Ahab and led the kingdom into deeper idolatry.

Since Jezebel was the wife of the reputed head of Israel, some commentators hold that Jezebel of Thyatira, although this is likely not her name, is the wife of the pastor.[22]

Because she is a prophetess, others hold this Jezebel may be a Thyatiran oracle or Sibyl.[23] There are several prophetesses mentioned in Scripture. See Exodus 15:20, Miriam; Judges 4:4, Deborah; 2 Kings 22:14, Huldah; Isaiah 8:3, Isaiah's wife; and Luke 2:36, Anna. There are also evil, false prophetesses such as Noadiah (Nehemiah 6:14).

In any event, this Jezebel typifies idolatry and heresy brought into the church. As Ramsey indicates, "Toleration of heresy is the characteristic of this church."[24] He goes on to say, "The whole epistle shows how great the evil is of tolerating in the church any teaching which has not the manifest stamp of Christ's authority upon it, no matter what may be its apparent wisdom or speciousness or harmlessness."[25]

Tolerance is the byword of modern culture. The sin of sins is intolerance. This spirit pervades the world and church. Biblical Christianity is viewed as too narrow. However, the way of Christ *is* narrow. "The gate is small and the way is narrow that leads to life" (Matthew 7:14).

Does Jezebel lead Thyatira into cultic idolatry, sensuality, and adultery? This may be the case. However, those "corrupting the church's purity and leading her members into a heinous spiritual adultery, are true Jezebels, with whatever attractions they may clothe themselves and their teachings . . . "[26] These Jezebels lead men and women down the broad way."The gate is wide and the way is broad that leads to destruction, and there are many who enter through it" (Matthew 7:13). All Jezebels and all who follow her need repentance.

Verse 21: "I gave her time to repent, and she does not want to repent of her immorality." Those who fail in the desire or inclination to repent are doomed. "For the mind set on the flesh is death" (Romans 8:6).

Verses 22-23 promise this judgment:

Behold, I will throw her on a bed of sickness and those who commit adultery with her into great tribulation, unless they repent of her deeds.

---

[22] Reid, 57.
[23] Swete, 43.
[24] Ramsey, 154.
[25] Ibid.
[26] Ibid., 155.

And I will kill her children with pestilence, and all the churches will know that I am He who searches the minds and hearts; and I will give to each one of you according to your deeds.

Christ will throw the adulterer into a *clinic*. Sickness and disease is incipient death. It is the doorway to eternal death for the unrepentant. In the end, all will acknowledge the Lordship of Christ (Philippians 2:10, Revelation 9:20-21).

Part Two

Christ proclaims judgment and doom upon those who follow Jezebel *and tolerate her*. The church is a mixed multitude (Exodus 12:38, Matthew 13:38). Christ therefore has words of encouragement for those in the congregation who are faithful, the rest.

Revelation 2:24, "But I say to you, the rest who are in Thyatira, who do not hold this teaching, who have not known the deep things of Satan, as they call them, I place no other burden on you."

We now glimpse into the heresy of Jezebel. It is characterized as "deep things of Satan." Some in the church disdain straightforward and objective truth. They seek esoteric, private, secret religion known only by a few. They are not content with what pertains to Christ and to salvation. They want something *deep*. Gnostic mysticism holds individuals can directly obtain such special knowledge outside of objective written revelation.

These people follow Satan rather than God. The things of God come to us through the revelation of Scripture. To walk by the Spirit means to follow the written word of God under the power of the Holy Spirit. Truth is objective not esoteric or hidden. We have no other burden than to seek out the truth of God in the word of God, in Scripture.

Satan tempts us to step outside of Scripture, to seek ultimate truth elsewhere, to consult psychics and readers. God says, "As for the person who turns to mediums and to spiritists, to play the harlot after them, I will also set My face against that person and will cut him off from among his people" (Leviticus 20:6).

What does Christ tell the faithful? "Nevertheless what you have, hold fast until I come" (verse 25). You have God's word and God's grace; hold fast until the end. Elsewhere Jesus promises, "The one who endures to the end, he will be saved" (Matthew 24:13). As already mentioned, we walk by the Spirit when we follow the word of God by the power of the Holy Spirit. This is what we have. To this we must hold fast at all cost.

King Saul experienced the work of the Spirit *upon* Him (1 Samuel 10:9-11). He was changed from a shepherd to a king, as was David, but Saul was not born again. Saul was a murderer (1 Samuel 19:9-10). "And you know that no murderer has eternal life abiding in him" (1 John 3:5). Scripture tells us, "the Spirit of the Lord departed from Saul, and an evil spirit from the Lord terrorized him" (1 Samuel 16:14). David remembered this departure of the Spirit all too

30

well. When he sinned with Bathsheba he feared the same egress of the Spirit. "Do not cast me away from Your presence and do not take Your Holy Spirit from me" (Psalm 51:11). The best assurance we are redeemed is holding fast until Christ comes to take us in death or to take us in His glorious second coming.

Verse 26: "He who overcomes, and he who keeps My deeds until the end, to him I will give authority over the nations." To overcome is to have victory. This is also the assurance we are born again. "For whatever is born of God overcomes the world; and this is the victory that has overcome the world—our faith" (1 John 5:4). We overcome the world when we follow the word of God and the law of God. We are enabled to do so by the Spirit. This is the way of faith.

The promise Christ gives believers comes from Psalm 2:7-9,

I will surely tell of the decree of the Lord:
He said to Me, "You are My Son,
Today I have begotten You.
Ask of Me, and I will surely give the nations as Your inheritance,
And the very ends of the earth as Your possession.
You shall break them with a rod of iron,
You shall shatter them like earthenware."

The Father promises to give Christ the nations, the very ends of the earth. The promise is fulfilled in the Great Commission and the spread of the gospel. Note two texts in particular. "Go therefore and make disciples of all the nations" (Matthew 28:19). "You shall be My witnesses both in Jerusalem, and in all Judea and Samaria, and even to the remotest part of the earth" (Acts 1:8).

As Believers, we participate in the fulfillment of this prophecy in two ways. First, we are caught up in the plan of God for the nations as we are converted and brought into His Kingdom. Second, the fulfillment advances as we propagate the gospel in our witness and our support of the gospel in prayer and in giving.

Verse 27: "And he shall rule them with a rod of iron, as the vessels of the potter are broken to pieces, as I also have received authority from My Father." How does this promise come to believers? Believers rule in the world only because Christ rules.

The reign of Christ is extended as believers live and proclaim the gospel and the law of God as His rule of righteousness. Christ reigns in the church as the word of God is faithfully proclaimed and the people of God follow Him as Lord. Christ rules in the world as the church proclaims the gospel and Christ subdues the hearts of men and women to Himself. Christ also rules in the world as believers faithfully carry out His dictates and follow His word. Finally, Christ rules in the exercise of His providence.

Christ exercises His rule in both blessing and judgment. "What if God, although willing to demonstrate His wrath and to make His power known, endured with much patience vessels of wrath prepared for destruction? And He did so to make known the riches of His glory upon vessels of mercy, which He prepared beforehand for glory" (Romans 9:22-23). Within the church, Christ exercises His reign as Saul-like and Jezebel-like people are disciplined. Such clay pots may experience the blows of Christ's strong scepter. If, under church discipline, they refuse to repent, they are headed for eternal destruction. They are broken.

Verse 28: "And I will give him the morning star." Those who live under and exercise Christ's rule receive the ultimate reward. The *morning star* is Christ (Revelation 22:16). Each tribe of Israel except one received a prescribed portion of the Promised Land. "Levi does not have a portion or inheritance with his brothers; the Lord is his inheritance" (Deuteronomy 10:9). Believers stand in the place of Levi. As David so eloquently put it, "My flesh and my heart may fail, but God is the strength of my heart and my portion forever" (Psalm 73:26).

Verse 29: "He who has an ear, let him hear what the Spirit says to the churches." We must listen with spiritual ears as well as physical ears.

The Letter to Sardis

Revelation 3:1-6

We have examined the letters to the three churches located in seaport communities along the Aegean: Ephesus in the south, Smyrna some thirty-five miles north, and Pergamum some fifty-five miles further northeast. We then moved inland about forty-five miles southeast to Thyatira.

Sardis is about thirty miles southeast of Thyatira. "For many ages this city had been celebrated for its wealth and magnificence. It was one of the most beautifully situated cities in all Asia."[27] "The city was addicted to a life of ease ... "[28] "The inhabitants of Sardis, we are told, were held in ill repute, even among the ancients, for their voluptuous habits of life."[29] "Like Thyatira, it was famous for its woolen manufacture and dyeing industry."[30]

Revelation 3:1, "To the angel of the church in Sardis write: He who has the seven Spirits of God and the seven stars, says this: 'I know your deeds, that you have a name that you are alive, but you are dead.'" Here is the gravest indictment made by Christ against the churches. On one side, this church has a name that it is alive.

We can make two points. "The members of the church in Sardis professed to be Christians, but they were in a state of sin, they were not Christians, their profession was but a name."[31] How often this proves to be the case. A profession of faith does not guarantee actual saving faith is resident within the heart (Matthew 7:22, 25:11).

But there is more to the indictment than the lives of individuals within the church. "The members of the church in Sardis had a name and a reputation for piety through all that region of country; they were celebrated as a model church; men pointed to them as an example in the management of church affairs, and in all the externals of religion . . . "[32]

"In all that man could see, this may have been a model church. The Lord does not charge her with any special sin. Her liberality and charity, her adherence to sound doctrine and morals, her observance of ordinances were all such that the mere superficial observer could see nothing to censure, but very much to praise."[33]

Yet, our Lord says to this church, "You are dead." This church is spiritually dead. There is formal and lifeless religion. "This is a most sad and perilous condition for any church to be found in; and yet it is a very frequent state of

---

[27] Ramsey, 163.
[28] Wilson, 41.
[29] Reid, 62
[30] Swete, 48.
[31] Reid, 63.
[32] Ibid.
[33] Ramsey, 164.

churches outwardly prosperous."[34]   Can this take place in orthodox Bible believing churches? Yes. There is such a thing as dead orthodoxy.

The exhortation to Sardis is simple and straightforward. Verse 2: "Wake up, and strengthen the things that remain, which were about to die; for I have not found your deeds completed in the sight of My God." The church that is dead, that is asleep, needs awakening. The words of Paul in Ephesians 5:14 apply. "Awake, sleeper, and arise from the dead, and Christ will shine on you."

How does awakening come?

> It usually requires, not only the reiterated warnings of God's word to be sounded in the ears, but generally some startling, crushing, humbling providences, to strike the stupid soul, and arouse it from its dreams of carnal security and worldly ease. Sickness, worldly losses, bitter disappointments, sore bereavements, or what is still worse, being left to fall into some open sin, are, one or more of them, the means used to awaken such, if there be any salvation for them.[35]

The command to wake up must accompany God's providences.

Certain things remain in the church in Sardis. The ordinances are present, the word, the sacraments, and prayer. Strengthen the use of these outward ordinances. The use of these means of grace is not perfect; they are incomplete. So often men, women, and pastors do not realize the design of God to work in power through these means of grace. In addition, we rarely see God's priority to use His visible church as an engine of mercy in the world. The church is, after all, the special dwelling place of God in the Spirit (Ephesians 2:22-23). We must therefore strengthen what remains.

Verse 3: "So remember what you have received and heard; and keep it, and repent." Therefore if you do not wake up, I will come like a thief, and you will not know at what hour I will come to you." Literally, the text reads, "Remember how you received and heard ... " Jesus reminds us how the word is often received. "The one on whom seed was sown on the rocky places, this is the man who hears the word and immediately receives it with joy" (Matthew 13:20). Did you receive the word with great joy upon your conversion? Was it a true and vital conversion based on the power of God (2 Corinthians 2:5)? Or are you too a rocky ground Christian having only temporary faith? David sinned gravely. He repented. David had saving faith. If you do not repent, judgment is sure. Christ will come as a thief and you will lose all.

Verse 4: "But you have a few people in Sardis who have not soiled their garments; and they will walk with Me in white, for they are worthy." A few people in the church are faithful and not simply formal in their relationship with God. They have the white robes of imputed righteousness. They are worthy to enter God's presence because of the work of Christ on their behalf.

---

[34] Ibid., 165.
[35] Ibid., 167-168.

Verse 5: "He who overcomes will thus be clothed in white garments; and I will not erase his name from the book of life, and I will confess his name before My Father and before His angels." The one who overcomes has vital faith (1 John 5:4). Reference to names not being erased assures us of the permanence of names in the Book of Life. Christ promises, "Therefore everyone who confesses Me before men, I will also confess him before My Father who is in heaven" (Matthew 10:32). Are we listening? Verse 6: "He who has an ear, let him hear what the Spirit says to the churches."

The Letter to Philadelphia

Revelation 3:7-13

Part One

About thirty miles south and east of Sardis, Philadelphia was a city frequently smitten by earthquakes. The church there was likely small. Only two of the churches among seven receive no censure, Smyrna and Philadelphia.

It is of some interest that the greater part of the visible church is worthy of condemnation. We dare not consider our own congregations to be above the common lot, above reproach. Christ knows our deeds and our hearts. On the other hand, we ought to strive to correct our deficiencies, as seen in five of the churches, and at the same time seek to emulate Smyrna and Philadelphia.

Revelation 3:7: "And to the angel of the church in Philadelphia write: He who is holy, who is true, who has the key of David, who opens and no one will shut, and who shuts and no one opens, says this." The *key of David* refers to the sovereign work of Christ. Matthew Henry rehearses the formidable nature of Christ's sovereignty over us:

> He opens a door of opportunity to his churches; he opens a door of utterance to his ministers; he opens a door of entrance, opens the heart; he opens a door of admission to the visible church, laying down the terms of communion; and he opens the door to the church triumphant, according to the terms of salvation fixed by him . . . When he pleases, he shuts the door of opportunity and the door of utterance, and leaves obstinate sinners shut up in the hardness of their hearts; he shuts the door of church fellowship against unbelievers and profane persons; and he shuts the door of heaven against the foolish virgins who have slept away their day of grace, and against the workers of iniquity, how vain and confident soever they may be.[36]

Christ commits the keys of the kingdom to His church: "I will give you the keys of the kingdom of heaven; and whatever you bind on earth shall have been bound in heaven, and whatever you loose on earth shall have been loosed in heaven" (Matthew 16:19). This is a great work. The promise to Philadelphia is that there is a door of service and ministry open to her. Verse 8: "I know your deeds. Behold, I have put before you an open door which no one can shut, because you have a little power, and have kept My word, and have not denied My name." This is a great promise.

Paul pleads for prayer "that God will open up to us a door for the word" (Colossians 4:3). He reports, "a wide door for effective service has opened to me" (1 Corinthians 16:9). And again, "When they had arrived and gathered the church together, they began to report all things that God had done with them and

---

[36] Matthew Henry, 6:1133.

how He had opened a door of faith to the Gentiles" (Acts 14:27). Philadelphia has an open door for service and ministry to advance the gospel.

The church may be small. There may be little power from a worldly perspective. Imagine the difference between Philadelphia and Sardis. The latter church had made a name for herself that she was a lively, active, ministering congregation, palpably blessed. But Christ said she was dead. Philadelphia, on the other hand, was a small struggling work, insignificant and obviously lacking in blessing from a worldly perspective. Christ says the door of ministry for the gospel is open to her.

Verse 9: "Behold, I will cause those of the synagogue of Satan, who say that they are Jews and are not, but lie—I will make them come and bow down at your feet, and make them know that I have loved you." So wide is the door open for ministry and service that the tables will be turned on the local religious establishment. The *synagogue of Satan* is a dwelling place of the evil one. It may manifest in different ways.

On one hand, the Jewish people saw themselves as chosen of God. They rejected the Messiah of God, Jesus Christ. They were not true Jews at all. Paul draws the line clearly. "For we are the true circumcision, who worship in the Spirit of God and glory in Christ Jesus and put no confidence in the flesh" (Philippians 3:3). He adds, "He is a Jew who is one inwardly; and circumcision is that which is of the heart, by the Spirit, not by the letter; and his praise is not from men, but from God." On the other hand, professing Christians often reject the Christ of the Bible. The Westminster Confession says, "The purest Churches under heaven are subject both to mixture and error; and some have so degenerated, as to become no Churches of Christ, but synagogues of Satan" (25:5).

Christ promises the Philadelphian Christians that both Jew and Gentile who disdain them will be constrained to worship before them. This may come about in two ways. Christ may exercise His rule and open their hearts to respond to the gospel proclaimed by these Christians. A door appears to be open by Christ for this. Or these persons will see Christ's love for the saints of Philadelphia on the Day of Judgment from outside the church. They will then be forced to bow before Christ (Philippians 2:10). God will display His love for His people one way or the other.

Verse 10: "Because you have kept the word of My perseverance, I also will keep you from the hour of testing, that hour which is about to come upon the whole world, to test those who dwell on the earth." A small faithful band of Christians can and often does have profound witness. Christ promises that, as testing and persecution come, these believers will be saved *through* the trials (1 Corinthians 10:13). The past keeping of the word of patience bodes well for future patient endurance. A reservoir of grace is found in the midst of testing. "If when you do what is right and suffer for it you patiently endure it, this finds favor with God" (1 Peter 2:20). The word translated *favor* is the word *grace*. If you have *favor* with God, you have *grace* from God. God's grace manifests most fully in our weakness.

This seems to be an aspect of Christianity many moderns miss. Paul gives us the same testimony (2 Corinthians 12:7-9). The synagogue of Satan may batter and buffet the saints in Philadelphia. We may receive the same treatment. Christ promises grace. We must persevere. Verse 11: "I am coming quickly; hold fast what you have, so that no one will take your crown."

Part Two

As mentioned above, the church at Philadelphia was one of the two churches out of seven, which received no word of condemnation. This does not mean the church was perfect. The two to five ratio does remind us praise without correction is rare. It is not the norm. We should therefore not think our congregations are above average and automatically fit in the category of Philadelphia.

In Revelation 3:11, Christ says to the church, "I am coming quickly; hold fast what you have, so that no one will take your crown." There are three ways in which to interpret the coming of Christ in this text. First, Christ may come in death. Jesus reminds us in John 14:1-3, "Do not let your heart be troubled; believe in God, believe also in Me. In My Father's house are many dwelling places; if it were not so, I would have told you; for I go to prepare a place for you. If I go and prepare a place for you, I will come again and receive you to Myself, that where I am, there you may be also."

Christ comes at death to receive the souls of those who belong to Him. His angels ascend with the souls of the saved (Genesis 28:12, John 1:51) and escort them into heaven (Luke 16:22). Christ may come at any time for us in this fashion. Psalm 139:16 exclaims, "In Your book were all written the days that were ordained for me, when as yet there was not one of them." Although this is the case, we must pray to God, "Teach us to number our days, that we may present to You a heart of wisdom" (Psalm 90:12). We do not know when we will be called upon to depart this veil of tears and enter glory.

Christ will also come a second time in glory to judge the earth. This day will come suddenly, unexpectantly, without warning. "For you yourselves know full well that the day of the Lord will come just like a thief in the night" (1 Thessalonians 5:2). Paul reminds the Thessalonian Christians, "But you, brethren, are not in darkness, that the day would overtake you like a thief" (1 Thessalonians 5:4). And Christ adds these telling words, "Be on guard, so that your hearts will not be weighted down with dissipation and drunkenness and the worries of life, and that day will not come on you suddenly like a trap" (Luke 21:34).

This day is unknown to all except the Father. He will send Christ at the time He has appointed. "But of that day and hour no one knows, not even the angels of heaven, nor the Son, but the Father alone" (Matthew 24:36).

Preparation is therefore of the utmost importance. "Therefore be on the alert, for you do not know which day your Lord is coming ... For this reason you also must be ready; for the Son of Man is coming at an hour when you do not think He will" (Matthew 24:42-44).

Finally, Christ visits the world with various judgments. Death is final. Christ's second coming ushers in the consummation of all things. As we await these final acts of God, Paul reminds us, "The wrath of God is revealed from heaven against all ungodliness and unrighteousness of men who suppress the truth in unrighteousness" (Romans 1:18).

As an example, because of their disobedience, Christ said to the Jewish nation and people, "Behold, your house is being left to you desolate!" (Matthew 23:38). Christ removed Israel's lampstand (Revelation 2:5) in 70 A.D. The judgments of God are warnings and calls to repentance (Revelation 9:20-21).

Churches should especially take heed today. You must "hold fast what you have, so that no one will take your crown." What do you have? You have the good news of the gospel of grace. You have the precious gift of the Holy Spirit. You have forgiveness on the basis of the work of Christ through faith in this Savior. You must persevere in this faith before God and never turn back to a trust in your own goodness or supposed good works. To do so is to risk the censure Paul gives the Galatians, "You have been severed from Christ, you who are seeking to be justified by law; you have fallen from grace" (Galatians 5:4).

The crown represents the rewards of grace. It is a crown of life; we are crowned with life (James 1:12). It is a crown of righteousness; we receive righteousness from Christ through faith (2 Timothy 4:8). To step back from the truth of justification by grace through faith is to forfeit the crown.

Christ therefore promises in verse 12, "He who overcomes, I will make him a pillar in the temple of My God, and he will not go out from it anymore; and I will write on him the name of My God, and the name of the city of My God, the New Jerusalem, which comes down out of heaven from My God, and My new name." We overcome through faith, an indication of our own emptiness and dependence upon God (1 John 5:4).

A pillar is a monument. The temple is the church. God makes believers monuments of grace within the church. These monuments are permanent. There is no going out. The Name on the monument is the Name of God and the name of the City of God. The temptation is to build empires, cities and names for ourselves. This was the fault of the people of ancient Babel (Genesis 11:4). We are not to make a city for ourselves or a name for ourselves.

The New Jerusalem is the spiritual body of Christ. Where the visible church and the spiritual body coincide, the church, New Jerusalem, *is coming down* out of heaven (Revelation 21:2). The church in the world is an outpost of heaven. We are citizens of heaven (Philippians 3:20). We are ambassadors from heaven for Christ (2 Corinthians 5:20). It is essential that men and women be incorporated into this spiritual body by the Holy Spirit (John 3:7, 1 Corinthians 12:13). One enters New Jerusalem only by way of Christ (John 14:6). Both the true nature of this spiritual body and the great Name of Christ must be set before the lost world. Believers bear the Name of Christ. They are Christians. They must therefore live as those who bear The Name. The letter ends with the familiar exhortation, "He who has an ear, let him hear what the Spirit says to the churches" (verse 13). Are *we* listening?

Christ Knocking

Revelation 3:20

Part One

Revelation 3:20 is of great interest and of supreme importance in the minds of many. For this reason, I am skipping ahead to expound this single text. My exposition of the great book of Revelation maintains the chief theme of this book is the majesty of God and of Jesus Christ, His Son. We will look at how the first three chapters of Revelation relate this in a wrap up of these chapters.

The ordinary way we come to grips with the majesty of God and of Christ is through the word of God and the application of that word to our hearts by the Holy Spirit. I maintain the best place for the Spirit-empowered word to take root in our hearts is within the worshipping community. Obviously personal Bible reading is not excluded. Neither do we exclude family worship.

The picture of the church used in Scripture is a temple. "The whole building, being fitted together, is growing into a holy temple in the Lord, in whom you also are being built together into a dwelling of God in the Spirit" (Ephesians 2:21-22). The presence of God in His temple differs from His presence elsewhere. We may speak of it this way. God is present in both heaven and hell. "If I ascend up into heaven, thou *art* there: if I make my bed in hell, behold, thou *art there.*" (Psalm 139:8, KJV). God is present in heaven in love and blessing. God is present in hell in wrath and judgment.

Francis Turretin describes the situation this way,

> God is far off from the wicked (as to the special presence of his favor and grace), but is always present with them by his general presence of essence. Where God is, there indeed is his grace originally and subjectively, but not always effectively because its exercise is perfectly free . . . Although he is differently in heaven and in hell (here by grace, there by justice; here as blessing, there as punishing), yet he can be in both places as to the immensity of his essence."[37]

Stephen Charnock adds:

> Good men have not only the essential presence, which is common to all, but his gracious presence; not only the presence that flows from his nature, but that which flows from his promise; his essential presence makes no difference between this and that man . . . ; his nature is the cause of the presence of his

---

[37] Francis Turretin, *Institutes of Elenctic Theology*, George Musgrave Giger, trans., James T. Dennison, ed., 3 vols. (Phillipsburgh, NJ: Presbyterian and Reformed Publishing, 1992), 1: 200.

essence; his will, engaged by his truth, is the cause of the presence of his grace."[38]

To what then do believers come as they gather for worship? Hebrews 12:18-23 declares:

> For you have not come to a mountain that can be touched and to a blazing fire, and to darkness and gloom and whirlwind . . . But you have come to Mount Zion and to the city of the living God, the heavenly Jerusalem, and to myriads of angels, to the general assembly and church of the firstborn who are enrolled in heaven, and to God, the Judge of all, and to the spirits of the righteous made perfect, and to Jesus, the mediator of a new covenant, and to the sprinkled blood.

When we worship with God's people, we enter the outer precincts of heaven:

> The gospel church is called mount Zion, the heavenly Jerusalem, which is free . . . This was the hill on which God set his king the Messiah. Now, in coming to mount Zion, believers come into heavenly places, and into a heavenly society . . . God has taken up his gracious residence in the gospel church, which on that account is an emblem of heaven . . . Here believers have clearer views of heaven, plainer evidences for heaven . . . [39]

Those who come to worship therefore enter the outer regions of heaven. R. B. Kuiper affirms,

> When God's people assemble for worship they enter into the places where God dwells. God meets them, and they meet God. They find themselves face to face with none other than God himself. Their worship is an intimate transaction between them and their God. If the church were fully conscience of that truth, what dignity and reverence would characterize its worship![40]

We should therefore desire Christ in our midst in worship. "Worship is special . . . The distinction between general service and specific worship can be illustrated by the fact of God's special presence."[41] James Bannerman teaches us:

> The outward provision of the visible church of Christ is mysteriously impregnated with Divine grace. The church itself is, in an especial and

---

[38] Stephen Charnock, *The Existence and Attributes of God* (Minneapolis: Klock and Klock Christian Publishers, 1977), 176.

[39] Matthew Henry, *Matthew Henry's Commentary, 6 vols.* (Westwood, NJ: Revell, n.d.), 6: 959.

[40] R.B.Kuiper,*The Glorious Body of Christ* (GrandRapids: Eerdmans Publishing Company, n.d.), 347.

[41] Frank J. Smith and David Lachman, eds., *Worship in the Presence of God* (Greenville, SC: Greenville Seminary Press, 1992), 12.

supernatural manner, the residence of the Holy Spirit; and in the right and faithful use of the ordinances the spirit of man meets the Spirit of God, and finds a blessing beyond the reach of ordinances.[42]

This is the overall biblical context of Revelation 3:20.

In addition, the text stands in a letter written to a specific church. The church at Laodicea is representative. We see a church in which Christ ought to richly dwell (Colossians 3:16, 4:16). The lesson we learn from her is therefore applicable to us. It ought to be taken to heart by us. We must relish Christ in our midst. We must cherish the voice of the Savior speaking to us as we worship together. We must treasure His holy oil fueling the lamps of our congregations to make us light in and to a sin-filled world.

Part Two

Jesus says to the church at Laodicea, "Behold, I stand at the door and knock; if anyone hears My voice and opens the door, I will come in to him and will dine with him, and he with Me" (Revelation 3:20). What is the door? Is Christ knocking at the door of the unbeliever's heart? This is a standard interpretation.

Geoffry Wilson says, "'Behold' is a summons to each individual to heed the promise of Christ, who condescends to stand at the heart's door and seek admittance."[43] Wilson then adds, "He not only knocks but also speaks and by his gracious words he awakens a responding love which enables the sinner to open the door and let him in."[44] Matthew Henry takes the same view:

> Here observe, [1.] Christ is graciously pleased by his word and Spirit to come to the door of the heart of sinners; he draws near to them in a way of mercy, ready to make them a kind visit. [2.] He finds this door shut against him; the heart of man is by nature shut up against Christ by ignorance, unbelief, and sinful prejudices. [3.] When he finds the heart shut, he does not immediately withdraw, but he waits to be gracious, even till his head be filled with the dew. [4.] He uses all proper means to awaken sinners, and to cause them to open to him: he calls by his word, he knocks by the impulses of his Spirit upon their conscience. [5.] Those who open to him shall enjoy his presence, to their great comfort and advantage . . . Alas! What do careless obstinate sinners lose by refusing to open the door of the heart to Christ![45]

Is this the proper view of the text? I do not think so. First, Jesus Christ is concluding His remarks to seven churches in seven letters. Each letter is addressed specifically to the angel of the respective church. Angels are

[42] James Bannerman, *The Church of Christ*, 2 vols. (Carlisle, PA: Banner of Truth, 1960), 1:89.

[43] Geoffrey Wilson, *Revelation* (Welwyn, England: Evangelical Press, 1985), 31.

[44] Ibid.

[45] Matthew Henry, *Matthew Henry's Commentary on the Whole Bible* (Westwood, NJ: Revell, n.d.), 6: 1136-1137.

messengers. Jesus calls John an angel (Mark 1:2, Luke 7:27, Greek New Testament); these angels are likely the pastors of the churches. Christ delivers His message to the church through His pastors and teachers (Ephesians 4:11). The pastors are also shepherds of local flocks. As we shall see, all of this has significance for our interpretation.

Second, Scripture never likens the heart to a door the sinner must open. If it is a door, Christ must open it. An example is the work of Christ when He opened Lydia's heart (Acts 16:14). Christ does this through the ministry of the word. He commissioned Paul to preach to the Gentiles and "to open their eyes so that they may turn from darkness to light and from the dominion of Satan to God" (Acts 26:18). William Holman Hunt's famous picture of Christ before a door is an interesting portrayal. As I recall, the door is hinged to swing toward Christ. When we open the front door in our homes to allow entrance, the door swings in. Not so the door in this picture. In addition, the latch is on Jesus' side of the door. Jesus must open this door.

Third, the language of the text does not carry with it the force of entering *into* the human heart. Perhaps this is too subtle. The verb used in the text is properly translated *come in*. The pronoun used indicates movement *toward*. The New American Standard Bible reads, "I will come in to him." The reference is to entering a room to dine with someone. The text does *not* say, "I will come *into* him." The original language does not bear this latter meaning.

To what does the door refer? The door is an entrance. Christ is outside the door. Based also upon the general biblical background given in Part I and other considerations to follow, I think the symbolism is clear. Christ is outside the door of this church. Christ is *outside* this church *not inside* in fellowship with the people. This is a serious indictment. The situation portrayed is all too common.

While teaching a Sabbath School class that had to do with worship, one of the elderly men said, "We do it right, we sing psalms; we have no problems." My response was simple. We are discussing spiritual matters here. We may have all the proper forms and the church can be sterile. Jesus put it this way, "This people honors Me with their lips, but their heart is far away from Me" (Matthew 15:8).

The Westminster Confession of Faith 25:5 reminds us some so-called churches are actually gathering places with Satan. "The purest Churches under heaven are subject both to mixture and error; and some have so degenerated, as to become no Churches of Christ, but synagogues of Satan." Recall Christ's words to the church at Smyrna.[46]

Why is Jesus at the door of the church at Laodicea? His presence may indicate impending judgment. "Do not complain, brethren, against one another, so that you yourselves may not be judged; behold, the Judge is standing right at the door" (James 5:9). The context of James 5:9 is quite similar to Revelation 3:20.

---

[46] See page 22.

44

The Laodiceans thought they were rich. They did not recognize their spiritual poverty. Jesus reproves them and calls them to repent. "Those whom I love, I reprove and discipline; therefore be zealous and repent" (Revelation 3:19). With this same reproof and call for repentance, Jesus says He is standing at the door. The message in James 5:9 is similar. Reject sin. Jesus is right at the door. In this context, we recall the words of Peter, "For it is time for judgment to begin with the household of God; and if it begins with us first, what will be the outcome for those who do not obey the gospel of God? (1 Peter 4:17). What of the church that is not a temple of the Holy Spirit? What of the church in which Christ does not dwell richly? Christ is at the door. Judgment is near.

Pastors and elders bear great responsibility before God in this matter. Elders should be desirous of hearing the word of God taught. They should be anxious that their pastors teach the whole counsel of God (Acts 20:26-27). The people should expectantly attend the public worship of God. They should listen to the word of God with anticipation. We should gather to draw near to God and to meet with God. We should gather for worship with Jesus Christ in our midst. *If He is not in our midst, He is outside knocking.*

Part Three

"Behold, I stand at the door and knock; if anyone hears My voice and opens the door, I will come in to him and will dine with him, and he with Me" (Revelation 3:20).

We said the door in our text symbolizes entrance to the church. Symbolically, Christ is outside the church. Jesus uses similar imagery in John 10:1-4:

Truly, truly, I say to you, he who does not enter by the door into the fold of the sheep, but climbs up some other way, he is a thief and a robber. But he who enters by the door is a shepherd of the sheep. To him the doorkeeper opens, and the sheep hear his voice, and he calls his own sheep by name and leads them out. When he puts forth all his own, he goes ahead of them, and the sheep follow him because they know his voice.

The faithful church of Jesus Christ is a sheepfold. As mentioned above, some sheepfolds become synagogues of Satan. This occurs when a thief enters the fold and subverts and deceives the sheep.

The Good Shepherd comes by way of the door. There is an under-shepherd who is a doorkeeper. Actual entrance into the fold is by the word of God proclaimed by the under-shepherd. He opens the door in his faithful teaching and preaching. Of course this assumes the blessing of Christ in the midst of the people of God as they worship together.

Scripture mixes metaphors. In John 10:1-4, the door is the entrance to the church as in Revelation 3:20. Christ enters through the door. However, the door is also Christ Himself. "Truly, truly, I say to you, I am the door of the sheep" (John 10:7). "I am the door; if anyone enters through Me, he will be saved, and will go in and out and find pasture" (John 10:9). This is not incompatible with the earlier figure of speech. I emphasize this simply to show the door is *not* the entrance to the sinner's heart.

The sayings of Jesus in John 10 are quite compatible with our interpretation of Revelation 3:20. In John 10, the sheep of the fold hear the voice of Jesus and follow Him. This is the need in Laodicea, "If anyone hears My voice," says Jesus. The great need of the church as a whole and of the individual members is to hear the voice of Christ. "My sheep hear My voice, and I know them, and they follow Me" (John 10:27).

We know there is hearing and then there is hearing. Jesus ends each of His letters in Revelation 2-3 with these telling words, "He who has an ear, let him hear what the Spirit says to the churches" (2:7, 11, 17, 29; 3:6, 13, 22). The letter to the Laodiceans, and to all of us, may be heard as it is read. But do we hear the voice of Jesus Christ in the words read? This seems to be a "Catch 22" situation. Christ is outside the church. Those inside need to truly hear the voice of the Savior. But only the sheep recognize the voice of the Good Shepherd.

Resolution comes in the faithful preaching and teaching of the word of God. Jesus promises, "I have other sheep, which are not of this fold; I must bring them also, and they will hear My voice; and they will become one flock with one shepherd" (John 10:16). Jesus must bring people into His flock. Individuals do not have the power in and of themselves to open their hearts to the word of God. Christ must open their hearts to the gospel (Acts 16:14). Christ must open their eyes to see Him as the Savior (Luke 24:31). Christ must open their minds to grasp the truth of God in Christ (Luke 24:45).

How does Christ do this? When Christ approaches the sheepfold, the faithful under-shepherd opens the door. Faith is dispensed in and through the word of God. "So faith comes from hearing, and hearing by the word of Christ" (Romans 10:17). This is the case because the new birth is sovereignly granted through, not independent of, the word of God. "For you have been born again not of seed which is perishable but imperishable, that is, through the living and enduring word of God" (1 Peter 1:23). This means the pastor must not only preach the word (2 Timothy 4:2), he must understand the work of the Spirit in sovereignly granting new birth through the word. This was Jesus' question to Nicodemus before he was born again. "Are you the teacher of Israel and do not understand these things?" (John 3:10). Not only do some teachers in the Israel of God not understand these things, they teach doctrines contrary to the word of God.

The letters to the seven churches are addressed to the angels, pastors, of these churches. These shepherds of local flocks have the duty and privilege of being doorkeepers. Faithful preaching and teaching opens the door to Christ. Men and women, young people and children may then gain spiritual ears from Christ. When they are born again, they hear the voice of the Good Shepherd. Heretical teaching, which serves the wisdom of men rather than the counsels of God, closes the door to Christ. Christ stands at the door and knocks. His presence indicates impending judgment.

Let's apply the text at this point on two levels. Jesus says, "Behold, I stand at the door and knock; if anyone hears My voice and opens the door . . . " Is there anyone who hears the voice of the shepherd? Does even the under-shepherd, the doorkeeper, know and hear His voice? Does he rush to open the door to communion with the Savior through the word of God and prayer and song?

I think of myself in this light. The Good Shepherd comes faithfully to meet with His people gathered for worship. Do I lead the people of God into His presence? Too often worship is a mere formality. It is a duty we accomplish, the sooner the better, and we are off to other things, the meal at home, and the afternoon nap. Am I conscious of my duty, my privilege, to open the door to Christ for the people gathered for worship? May God grant me grace in this regard.

What about the congregation? When Jesus enters the sheepfold, He calls the sheep by name (John 10:3). Do the people hear Jesus call them each by name? Or is this an empty figure of speech? The Good Shepherd cares for His sheep (Ezekiel 34:12). He surveys the flock. He assists the wounded and injured (Isaiah 61:1; Psalm 23:5). We should purposely gather for worship to meet with Jesus, to hear His voice, to greet Immanuel, God with us (Matthew 1:23).

Part Four

"Behold, I stand at the door and knock; if anyone hears My voice and opens the door, I will come in to him and will dine with him, and he with Me" (Revelation 3:20).

When the door of the word of God is opened, Christ enters freely into the midst of His people and dwells among them. The people of God follow the injunction of James 4:8: "Draw near to God and He will draw near to you." Matthew Henry exhorts, "Draw nigh to God, in his worship and institutions, and in every duty he requires of you."[47]

This was the perspective of the Old Testament saints. Sinning Levites were warned not to draw near to God in ceremonial worship. They faced judgment. "And they shall not come near to Me to serve as a priest to Me, nor come near to any of My holy things, to the things that are most holy; but they will bear their shame and their abominations which they have committed" (Ezekiel 44:13). In like manner, as James exhorts us to draw near to God, he also warns, "Cleanse your hands, you sinners; and purify your hearts, you double-minded" (James 4:8).

Exodus 19:22 is similar. "Let the priests who come near to the Lord consecrate themselves, or else the Lord will break out against them" (Exodus 19:22). We are all priests of God (Revelation 1:6). We must all draw near to

---

[47] Matthew Henry, *Matthew Henry's Commentary on the Whole Bible* (Westwood, NJ: Revell, n.d.), 6: 990.

God in His spiritual temple, the church. This is His *special* dwelling place on the earth.

Why should we draw near to God in worship? We draw near for salvation. "He [Christ] is able also to save forever those who draw near to God through Him, since He always lives to make intercession for them" (Hebrews 7:25). We draw near to gain mercy and grace. "Let us draw near with confidence to the throne of grace, so that we may receive mercy and find grace to help in time of need" (Hebrews 4:16). We may only draw near through our faith in Christ. "Let us draw near with a sincere heart in full assurance of faith, having our hearts sprinkled clean from an evil conscience and our bodies washed with pure water" (Hebrews 10:22).

My point is that the true sheepfold never shuns Christ but heeds the Savior and draws near to Him. The church at Laodicea was in a dangerous position because it had no will to draw near to God. However, if we draw near to God through Christ, the promise is God will draw near to us. Jesus says to the church, "If anyone hears My voice and opens the door, I will come in to him and will dine with him, and he with Me." Christ will not be outside the church, knocking and threatening judgment. He will be inside the church animating the body, giving life to the body.

The result is the church's fellowship with Christ. In fact, Jesus promises intimate table fellowship. Matthew 22:1-4:

> Jesus spoke to them again in parables, saying, "The kingdom of heaven may be compared to a king who gave a wedding feast for his son. And he sent out his slaves to call those who had been invited to the wedding feast, and they were unwilling to come. Again he sent out other slaves saying, 'Tell those who have been invited, "Behold, I have prepared my dinner; my oxen and my fattened livestock are all butchered and everything is ready; come to the wedding feast."'"

Fellowship with Christ is pictured as a feast, a banquet, and a wedding celebration. Family fellowship around the table is a time for family conversation, planning, and counsel. It is no different with God's family. We draw near to Him for communion with Him. We draw near to dine with Christ and to feast on His word. We seek His face in corporate worship to gain counsel and be sustained Him.

Communion with Christ is epitomized in the fellowship of the Lord's Supper. Here we find union and communion with Christ on its highest earthly plane. Our greatest privilege is not voting on the church budget. Participation in the Lord's Supper is our highest privilege. This is why we have *communicant* church membership. This is why the unrepentant, rendered unworthy because of sinful conduct, are ex*communicated*. Jesus says in Revelation 3:20, "I will come in to him and will dine with him, and he with Me."

Why does Jesus use the singular at this point rather than the plural? I think He does so for an important reason. We may have our most personal and pointed encounters with Christ in the corporate setting. If the church is the temple of the Spirit where God is present in an especially gracious manner, the result will be profound, intimate and personal communion and fellowship with Him.

In addition, during the Lord's Supper each individual partakes of the bread and drinks of the cup. He or she dines with Christ. By faith there is a feasting on the true bread of heaven (John 6:51). There is an intimate abiding in the vine (John 15:5). We are fed for our arduous journey in the wilderness of this life just as Israel was nourished by manna. Jesus says, "Our fathers ate the manna in the wilderness; as it is written, 'He gave them bread out of heaven to eat'" (John 6:31). Jesus goes on to say, "I am the living bread that came down out of heaven; if anyone eats of this bread, he will live forever; and the bread also which I will give for the life of the world is My flesh" (John 6:51). In Revelation 3:20, He promises, "I will come in to him and will dine with him, and he with Me."

This fellowship with Christ as He dwells among us and walks in our midst in worship, this communion epitomized in the Lord's Supper, is a foretaste of heaven. This is true because the church is the threshold of heaven (Psalm 84:10). When we gather, we come to the "heavenly Jerusalem" (Hebrews 12:22). Therein we have a taste of the age to come (Hebrews 6:5). We anticipate the wedding feast of the Lamb (Revelation 19:7). Jesus Christ is in our midst. We hear His voice in the reading of Scripture, in the singing of Psalms, and in the preaching of His word. The words of Jesus are fulfilled, "I will come in to him and will dine with him, and he with Me."

Where is Jesus Christ with reference to our congregations? By God's grace, He is not outside the church. In the proper use of the means of grace, Christ is present in the midst of our worshipping body. Revelation 3:20 points us to His gracious presence with us.

The Letter to Laodicea

Revelation 3:14-22

Part One

The position I take regarding Revelation is that it is divided into seven parts. Each section recapitulates the period between the first coming of Christ and His second coming from a different perspective. In addition, as we move through the book, more emphasis is placed upon the circumstances surrounding the second coming of Christ whereas the first section views circumstances close to the first advent. This sevenfold approach gives us a complete and adequate view of the interadvent period.

The number seven is also prominent in section one. The letters to the seven churches give us a comprehensive, complete and adequate view of the church. The letter to the church at Laodicea does not represent the church in this latter age, close to the second coming. Rather, combined with the other letters, it pictures the church in all ages.

Revelation 3:14: "To the angel of the church in Laodicea write: The Amen, the faithful and true Witness, the Beginning of the creation of God, says this." Again, the angel is the messenger of God among God's people. This is the pastor of the church. He receives the Word of God from Christ and is responsible for faithfully transmitting it to the church.

Laodicea is about fifty miles south and east of Ephesus. Wilson notes, "Prosperous Laodicea was famous for its banks, its clothing and carpets made from the local glossy black wool and its medical school which produced a noted ear ointment and eye salve (v. 18)."[48]

Christ shows Himself as the Beginning of creation. The word translated *beginning* is the root for our word architect. Christ is the designer and fabricator of creation. This is not a text showing Christ to be a creature. Far from it, Christ is the origin and source of creation. Christ gives Laodicea the sharpest of the rebukes given to the churches.

Verse 15: "I know your deeds, that you are neither cold nor hot; I wish that you were cold or hot." It is always best not to be fanatical. Correct? Moderation is the byword. This life calls for moderation in all things. This is not the case according to Jesus Christ. Christ is not looking for moderation. He is especially not looking for moderation in faith and life. "I wish that you were cold or hot." It would be far better that you were either red-hot or ice cold than merely tepid. One thing we despise is tepid coffee or tea. So it is with Christianity. Christ commended John the Baptizer for his white-hot zeal. "He was the lamp that was burning and was shining and you were willing to rejoice for a while in his light" (John 5:35).

---

[48] Geoffrey Wilson, *Revelation* (Welwyn: Evangelical Press, 1985), 48.

Verse 16: "So because you are lukewarm, and neither hot nor cold, I will spit you out of My mouth." The word translated *spit* is rendered *vomit* in the margin of the New American Standard Bible. The picture is vivid.

I once tried to illustrate this text to a group of high school students. I placed a chair in the front of the platform to represent a toilet. I threw myself in front of the chair and began to wretch. My effort was to portray what we sometimes call the heaves. We end in dry heaves. Our bodies reject the contents of our stomachs. The demonstration must have been a success. When I turned around and sat in the chair the small auditorium was filled with groans of disgust.

This is the whole point. Christ is filled with disgust for the church at Laodicea. He says this church is tepid. The church makes Him wretch. The very thought of this church makes Him ill.

What of our congregations? Are we luke-warm? Are we too content with moderation before God and Christ? Do we speak against sin? Do we declare the wrath of God against sin? Are we full of compassion for the lost? Do we proclaim the verities of Christ fully, without reservation or shame? Perhaps political correctness carries the day rather than biblical correctness. Perhaps a desire not to offend rules our thinking.

The words of the apostle Paul ring clear and true. "Am I now seeking the favor of men, or of God? Or am I striving to please men? If I were still trying to please men, I would not be a bond-servant of Christ" (Galatians 1:10). Being a man-pleaser is incompatible with service to Christ. Hence the indictment against luke-warmness. Of course, we must extend common courtesies to all people. These are the courtesies due to others because they bear the image of God. "Love your enemies and pray for those who persecute you"; and "Love your enemies, do good to those who hate you" (Matthew 5:44, Luke 6:27). At the same time we must speak the truth. As we do so, we must speak the truth with love (Ephesians 4:15).

The problem with the Laodiceans was their apparent wealth and the apparent blessing of God attending that wealth. Verse 17: "Because you say, 'I am rich, and have become wealthy, and have need of nothing,' and you do not know that you are wretched and miserable and poor and blind and naked."

The riches of Laodicea were material. Such is the case with many people today. Too often, outward wealth is taken as an undoubted indication of spiritual blessing. Even God's covenant blessings have two sides. Look at the situation with Isaac and Ishmael. Genesis 21:9-13 and 20:

Now Sarah saw the son of Hagar the Egyptian, whom she had borne to Abraham, mocking. Therefore she said to Abraham, "Drive out this maid and her son, for the son of this maid shall not be an heir with my son Isaac." The matter distressed Abraham greatly because of his son. But God said to Abraham, "Do not be distressed because of the lad and your maid; whatever Sarah tells you, listen to her, for through Isaac your descendants shall be named. And of the son of the maid I will make a nation also, because he is your descendant." . . . God was with the lad . . .

Ishmael was blessed in a tangible and material way because of his connection to Abraham. *Outward* benefits of the covenant were his. The *spiritual* benefits of the covenant were not his. God said to Abraham, "Through Isaac your descendants shall be named." *Physical blessing* does not necessarily indicate *spiritual blessing*. Those of Laodicea thought differently. "I am rich, and have become wealthy, and have need of nothing."

Part Two

The church at Laodicea was deceived. The people thought their material wealth indicated eternal security. Such was not the case. Christ speaks pointedly, "I advise you to buy from Me gold refined by fire so that you may become rich, and white garments so that you may clothe yourself, and that the shame of your nakedness will not be revealed; and eye salve to anoint your eyes so that you may see" (Revelation 3:18). We dare not be similarly deceived. We need to take the advice of Christ.

Real wealth is eternal. God refines your faith like precious metal so that "the proof of your faith, being more precious than gold which is perishable, even though tested by fire, may be found to result in praise and glory and honor at the revelation of Jesus Christ" (1 Peter 1:7). With faith intact, you inherit real wealth.

White garments are white with the righteousness of Christ. This is the perfect life lived by Christ on behalf of His people. God says, "So you shall keep My statutes and My judgments, by which a man may live if he does them; I am the Lord" (Leviticus 18:5). Christ did what we are unable to do. Christ fulfilled the requirements of the Law and procured life. Because His works are of infinite value as the Son of God, these same good works purchase heaven for all those who trust in Him, all the elect.

We *purchase* these white garments, not with our works. Jesus accomplished all. We purchase these white garments by abandoning hope and reliance in self and trusting solely in the work of Christ.

If we do not trust Christ, the shame of our nakedness will be revealed. When Adam and Eve sinned against God, "The eyes of both of them were opened, and they knew that they were naked" (Genesis 3:7). Their nakedness was both physical *and* spiritual. They were without clothes. They were without a covering for their sin. Hebrews 4:13 says, "There is no creature hidden from His sight, but all things are open and laid bare to the eyes of Him with whom we have to do." So it is for all of us. Matthew Henry observes, "We have reason to be afraid of approaching to God if we are not clothed and fenced with the righteousness of Christ, for nothing but this will be armour of proof and cover the shame of our nakedness."[49]

---

[49] Matthew Henry, *Matthew Henry's Commentary on the Whole Bible* (Nutley, NJ: Revell, n.d.), 1:27.

Nakedness, a symbol of sin, was not permitted at God's altar. The Lord commanded Moses; "You shall not go up by steps to My altar, so that your nakedness will not be exposed on it" (Exodus 20:26). The nakedness of sin must be covered with the righteousness of Christ.

At the same time, where there is sin, there ought to be shame. We should understand that it is far better for us to experience deep shame for sin in this life rather than in the life to come. In this life there is opportunity for repentance. In the life to come there is no such opportunity. There is only punishment for sin. "Now, little children, abide in Him, so that when He appears, we may have confidence and not shrink away from Him in shame at His coming" (1 John 2:28). Hell is a place of deep and abiding shame from which there is no release for all eternity. The shame of sinners will be revealed to all but most fully to themselves.

The Laodiceans also needed more than eye salve made in their own clinics. They needed spiritual eyes. They needed eyes open to the spiritual truths of the Word of God. Recall the disciples on the Emmaus road after the Passion of Christ. "While they were talking and discussing, Jesus Himself approached and began traveling with them. But their eyes were prevented from recognizing Him. Later, when the risen Christ broke bread with them, "then their eyes were opened and they recognized Him" (Luke 24:31).

Were the eyes of the Laodiceans prevented from recognizing spiritual things? Did their affluence blind them? "A natural man does not accept the things of the Spirit of God, for they are foolishness to him; and he cannot understand them, because they are spiritually appraised" (1 Corinthians 2:14). Were their eyes blinded by Satan? "The god of this world has blinded the minds of the unbelieving so that they might not see the light of the gospel of the glory of Christ, who is the image of God" (2 Corinthians 4:4). Christ must open their eyes.

One way He does this is through reproof. Reproof for sin is therefore a sign of the love of God. Verse 19: "Those whom I love, I reprove and discipline; therefore be zealous and repent." The thought comes from Proverbs 3:12, "For whom the Lord loves He reproves, even as a father corrects the son in whom he delights." The writer to the Hebrews reminds his readers suffering under persecution is a form of discipline; it manifests the love of God (Hebrews 12:4-13).

Reproof is often needed in the church. Paul tells Timothy, "Preach the word; be ready in season and out of season; reprove, rebuke, exhort, with great patience and instruction" (2 Timothy 4:2). It is the Word of God that is fit for such activity. "All Scripture is inspired by God and profitable for teaching, for reproof, for correction, for training in righteousness" (2 Timothy 3:16).

Verse 20: "Behold, I stand at the door and knock; if anyone hears My voice and opens the door, I will come in to him and will dine with him, and he with Me." Christ stands at the door of the church in judgment, the third scenario suggested in the exposition of Revelation 3:11. Christ is outside the church in judgment where faith, the righteousness of Christ, and spiritual eyesight are all absent. See the previous exposition.[50] Compare verse 17.

Verse 21 relates God's promise to those who heed the reproof. "He who overcomes, I will grant to him to sit down with Me on My throne, as I also overcame and sat down with My Father on His throne." Only faith born of the Spirit overcomes the world (1 John 5:4). To sit with Christ on the Father's throne is to rule with Christ (Revelation 20:4). Pastors rule with Christ when they preach the Word of God. Elders reign with Christ when they guide the church with the rule of His Word. Believers rule with Christ when they implement His Word in their homes, work places, and within the general culture. Are we listening? Verses 22 and 19: "He who has an ear, let him hear what the Spirit says to the churches." "Be zealous therefore, and repent."

---

[50] See above on pages 36 and 37.

Apprehension of the Majesty of Christ

One of the objectives of reading the Bible, of knowing God and of worshipping together is to obtain an adequate understanding of the majesty of Christ. This is true of the Book of Revelation. As we read this great book, we must come to grips with the majesty of Christ. This is one of the great themes of the book. I think this is also one of the blessings promised to us, "Blessed is he who reads and those who hear the words of the prophecy, and heed the things which are written in it" (Revelation 1:3). This is certainly one of the great lessons for the churches in chapters 2 and 3.

As we have noted, Revelation begins with a greeting, a description of Christ, and John's reaction to Him. Revelation 1:4-5: "John to the seven churches that are in Asia: Grace to you and peace, from Him who is and who was and who is to come, and from the seven Spirits who are before His throne, and from Jesus Christ, the faithful witness, the firstborn of the dead, and the ruler of the kings of the earth."

Revelation 1:12-16:

> Then I turned to see the voice that was speaking with me. And having turned I saw seven golden lampstands; and in the middle of the lampstands I saw one like a son of man, clothed in a robe reaching to the feet, and girded across His chest with a golden sash. His head and His hair were white like white wool, like snow; and His eyes were like a flame of fire. His feet were like burnished bronze, when it has been made to glow in a furnace, and His voice was like the sound of many waters. In His right hand He held seven stars, and out of His mouth came a sharp two-edged sword; and His face was like the sun shining in its strength.

In each of the letters to the seven churches, Christ immediately refers to these descriptions and visions. These churches must grasp the majesty of the Lord, King, and Head of the church.

Revelation 2:1: "The One who holds the seven stars in His right hand, the One who walks among the seven golden lampstands, says this." The ever present and omnipresent Majestic One upholds the ministry of His church.

Revelation 2:8: "The first and the last, who was dead, and has come to life, says this." The Majestic One reveals the eternal character of His life in resurrection.

Revelation 2:12: "The One who has the sharp two-edged sword says this." The Majestic One comes with the Word of consummate blessing and judgment.

Revelation 2:18: "The Son of God, who has eyes like a flame of fire, and His feet are like burnished bronze, says this." Know this: the eyes of the Majestic One pierce the heart and His steps are sure.

Revelation 3:1: "He who has the seven Spirits of God and the seven stars, says this." The Majestic One possesses the Spirit of perfection. He upholds His ministry with this Spirit of perfect power.

Revelation 3:7: "He who is holy, who is true, who has the key of David, who opens and no one will shut, and who shuts and no one opens, says this." The majesty of Christ includes perfect holiness. He alone opens heaven to some and closes eternal bliss to others. He does so with perfect justice and righteousness. Revelation 3:14: "The Amen, the faithful and true Witness, the Beginning of the creation of God, says this." The Majestic Christ is the Amen, the final Word of God, and the architect of truth.

Churches and individuals must come to grips with the majesty of God, the Creator, and Christ, the Redeemer. Christ introduces Himself to each congregation, relating His majestic power and glory, to emphasize this. We take it as central to Christianity, if men and women are to properly serve Christ, God must press home to their hearts the greatness of this Majestic One.

For this reason too, the message of each letter corresponds to the revelation or vision of Christ given to that church. In Ephesus, there is a loss of love. Christ reveals Himself as the One who is the fulfillment of covenant love. He walks in the midst of the church.

In Smyrna, the danger is fear of impending persecution. Christ manifests Himself as victor over death itself. Do not fear! In Pergamum, Christ detects worldliness infiltrating the church. Christ shows Himself as the One with both the word of blessing and the sword of judgment. In Thyatira, the church tolerated heresy while others in her midst rejected these false teachings. Christ shows Himself with feet of bronze fully able to sternly tread the wine press of wrath. He has the power to rule. Some reign with Him as they implement His Word.

In Sardis, the problem was a good reputation with no life from the Spirit. Christ has the only Spirit, the perfect Spirit, from whom we must gain strength and life. Esprit de corps may win favor with the world but it is not the Spirit of God. Philadelphia has an open door of ministry and service before her. Christ therefore displays Himself as the One who wields the Key of David. He has the ultimate power to open and close heaven. Finally, in Laodicea, the problem is luke-warmness. Christ makes himself known as the Amen. There is nothing tepid in God's exclamation point.

Churches and individuals must know the majestic attributes of Christ whether gracious or judgmental. We sometimes demur at the thought of doctrine. The attributes of Christ display His person. We fail to know Him if we do not understand or recognize His attributes. How is it possible to serve the Christ we confess without an appreciation of his Majesty? The Book of Revelation and the pictures of Christ given to the seven churches answer the question plainly. We cannot.

God impresses us with the majesty of Christ to change our hearts, alter our behavior, and temper our attitudes. When John saw the vision of Christ, his heart failed. Christ raised him up. Revelation 1:17: "When I saw Him, I fell at His feet like a dead man. And He placed His right hand on me, saying, 'Do not be afraid; I am the first and the last.'" The same was true on the Sea of Galilee. "When the disciples saw Him walking on the sea, they were terrified, and said,

'It is a ghost!' And they cried out in fear. But immediately Jesus spoke to them, saying, 'Take courage, it is I; do not be afraid'" (Matthew 14:26-27). The church needs to hear the Word of Christ. The church also needs an apprehension of the greatness and majesty of Christ.

The Throne Room of God

Revelation 4

The book of Revelation impresses us with the greatness of God and the majesty of Christ. The visions engender deep reverence and awe before the Almighty. They produce assurance regarding the victory of Christ and the gospel. The exposition now takes us, with Revelation 4, where Christ leads us, into the throne room of God.

"After these things I looked, and behold, a door standing open in heaven, and the first voice which I had heard, like the sound of a trumpet speaking with me, said, 'Come up here, and I will show you what must take place after these things'" (verse 1).

In this magnificent vision John sees a door standing open in heaven. We must remember John is granted an extraordinary view of things in the preternatural world. As John sees this open door a voice from heaven beckons him. Only a slice of glory is visible through the door. More is promised. "Immediately I was in the Spirit; and behold, a throne was standing in heaven, and One sitting on the throne" (verse 2).

Through the door John sees a throne, the throne of heaven. There is one sitting on the throne. John instinctively knows who He is. So do we. "And He who was sitting was like a jasper stone and a sardius in appearance; and there was a rainbow around the throne, like an emerald in appearance" (verse 3).

No specific description is given of the One who sits on the throne. He is like a jasper stone. Probably a clear and translucent gem representing God's absolute moral purity and holiness. He is also like a fiery red sardius representing the judgmental side of God's infinitely perfect character. Around the throne we see the emerald glow of a rainbow reminding us of God's covenantal character (Genesis 9:13). "Around the throne were twenty-four thrones; and upon the thrones I saw twenty-four elders sitting, clothed in white garments, and golden crowns on their heads" (verse 4).

Many expositors think these elders represent the saints throughout the ages. In part, this is a position based upon the translation of late Greek manuscripts of Revelation 5:9. The four living creatures and the elders sing together: "Thou art worthy to take the book, and to open the seals thereof: for thou wast slain, and hast redeemed *us* to God by thy blood out of every kindred, and tongue, and people, and nation" (KJV, italics added).

If we follow this reading, the elders must be a representative body of believers in heaven. The better reading excludes *us*. "Worthy are You to take the book and to break its seals; for You were slain, and purchased for God with Your blood men from every tribe and tongue and people and nation." For this reason and because one of the elders references others, outside the circle of the twenty-four, as glorified saints (Revelation 7:13-14), I think these elders are a rank in the hierarchy of angels. Compare Colossians 1:16.

"Out from the throne come flashes of lightning and sounds and peals of thunder. And there were seven lamps of fire burning before the throne, which are the seven Spirits of God" (verse 5).

Alford observes, in connection with Revelation 11:19, this lightning and thunder are "the solemn salvos, so to speak, of the artillery of heaven." Anyone present when a dignitary is given a twenty-one gun salute understands the imagery. Heavenly power salutes its Sovereign.

We also see seven great lights surrounding the throne. This is the Spirit of God, the Spirit of burning Holiness, illumining heaven with perfect light. Seven is the number of perfection. "And before the throne there was something like a sea of glass, like crystal; and in the center and around the throne, four living creatures full of eyes in front and behind" (verse 6).

The throne sits on a vast sea. This sea is smooth as glass and clear as crystal. The sea in Revelation often represents humanity. It is often a boiling cauldron (Revelation 13:1, 17:15; Daniel 7:2-3; and Isaiah 17:12). The sovereign sway of the Almighty brings calm to the sea of humanity. I emphasize this is a *vast sea*. It extends to infinity in every direction. God's power sets the cosmos in order.

There are four great and striking creatures around the throne. They have eyes all over, within and without, representing their pervasive vision and knowledge of the things of God. These are great angelic beings attending the throne of God.

> The first creature was like a lion, and the second creature like a calf, and the third creature had a face like that of a man, and the fourth creature was like a flying eagle. And the four living creatures, each one of them having six wings, are full of eyes around and within; and day and night they do not cease to say, "Holy, holy, holy is the Lord God, the Almighty, who was and who is and who is to come" (Verses 7-9).

This scene reminds us of the vision of Isaiah 6 and the song of seraphim. Surely these living beings are the highest rank of angels standing guard before the throne. They have great dignity. The lion is power. The ox is wisdom. The third is prototype man. The eagle is swiftness. Their threefold song of holiness indicates God is the holiest of all. Their continual singing signifies God's unceasing definitive holiness.

> And when the living creatures give glory and honor and thanks to Him who sits on the throne, to Him who lives forever and ever, the twenty-four elders will fall down before Him who sits on the throne, and will worship Him who lives forever and ever, and will cast their crowns before the throne, saying, "Worthy are You, our Lord and our God, to receive glory and honor and power; for You created all things, and because of Your will they existed, and were created" (Verses 10-11).

The angels acknowledge their authority comes from God; they cast their crowns before the throne. Only God, the Almighty, is worthy to receive all honor and power and glory. Only God is worthy. No other creature in the universe dare make this claim. The majesty of the Almighty makes this abundantly clear.

Exalt the Lamb, Exult in the Book

Revelation 5

Our central purpose is to come to grips with the glory of God and the majesty of Jesus Christ as we witness the awesome power of Christ to set the plans and purposes of God in motion. John is in God's throne room. "I saw in the right hand of Him who sat on the throne a book written inside and on the back, sealed up with seven seals" (verse 1).

The hand of God is outstretched. In His open palm John sees a book. It is sealed with seven seals. This book is a closed book, perfectly sealed. It is the book of God's decrees, His eternal plans and solemn purposes. The book is written inside and out showing the comprehensive character of God's sovereign plans.

"And I saw a strong angel proclaiming with a loud voice, 'Who is worthy to open the book and to break its seals?'" (verse 2). A mighty angel asks all heaven if anyone is able to open the book. Brute strength is not the precondition. Rather, moral purity and ethical integrity are the prime qualifications. Holiness is the prerequisite. John declares this solemn reality. "And no one in heaven or on the earth or under the earth was able to open the book or to look into it (verse 3).

No angel, great or small, is *worthy* to open the book. No heavenly being can take his stand before God and make such a claim. No earthly creature is likewise able. Fallen humanity is totally disqualified, *unworthy*. Can the nether world produce someone? Never! The leader of the underworld, Satan himself, does not qualify. That malignant being can act only at the behest of the Almighty. May we all realize this is the case.

John's reaction is startling, "Then I began to weep greatly because no one was found worthy to open the book or to look into it" (verse 4). Because no creature in the universe is found worthy to open the mysteries of God, John weeps. Oh that more of God's people would have such heartfelt conviction concerning the mysteries of God and a desire to know Him.

"And one of the elders said to me, 'Stop weeping; behold, the Lion that is from the tribe of Judah, the Root of David, has overcome so as to open the book and its seven seals'" (verse 5). This elder reminds us of two ancient prophecies concerning Christ.

When Jacob blessed his twelve sons, he said, "Judah is a lion's whelp . . . The scepter shall not depart from Judah, nor the ruler's staff from between his feet" (Genesis 49:9-10). Jesus Christ is the Lion of Judah. He is the One of whom it is written, "Then a shoot will spring from the stem of Jesse, and a branch from his roots will bear fruit (Isaiah 11:1). The Root of David is worthy.

"And I saw between the throne (with the four living creatures) and the elders a Lamb standing, as if slain, having seven horns and seven eyes, which are the seven Spirits of God, sent out into all the earth" (verse 6).

Literally John sees the Lamb in the middle of the throne. Hardly another book in the New Testament emphasizes the deity of Christ the way Revelation does. Christ is in the throne with God the Father. He is equal with Him in glory and honor.

The Lion who is a Lamb is startling in appearance. The lamb was slain yet He lives. He stands in triumph. He has seven horns. The horn represents power. This Lamb's power is *perfect* and *comprehensive*. The Lamb also has seven eyes. He has perfect sight and perfect knowledge. Again, we meet the seven Spirits of God. God does not actually have seven Spirits. The Spirit of Christ is the *perfect* Spirit of the Almighty and Holy God.

Because of the worthiness of His life and death, John says of the Lamb, "And He came and took the book out of the right hand of Him who sat on the throne" (verse 7). The Lamb within the throne relieves the Father of the book and prepares to disclose the purposes of God. What is the result of this seemingly simple action?

"When He had taken the book, the four living creatures and the twenty-four elders fell down before the Lamb, each one holding a harp and golden bowls full of incense, which are the prayers of the saints" (verse 8).

The Lamb takes the book and the highest courts of heaven prostrate themselves in worship. The incense of prayer rises before the throne. The melody of praise, symbolized by the harps, comes before the Lamb in the middle of the throne.

> And they sang a new song, saying, "Worthy are You to take the book and to break its seals; for You were slain, and purchased for God with Your blood men from every tribe and tongue and people and nation. You have made them to be a kingdom and priests to our God; and they will reign upon the earth" (Verses 9-10).

The angels were at a loss concerning the full purposes of God set forth by the prophets. What the prophets spoke represented "things into which angels long to look" (1 Peter 1:12). When the angels begin to see the magnificent works of God, they sing the old song of redemption with *new* vigor born of *new* understanding. They see the Christ about to erect His kingdom with the power of an indestructible life (Hebrews 7:16).

> Then I looked, and I heard the voice of many angels around the throne and the living creatures and the elders; and the number of them was myriads of myriads, and thousands of thousands, saying with a loud voice, "Worthy is the Lamb that was slain to receive power and riches and wisdom and might and honor and glory and blessing" (Verses 11-12).

All the heavenly angelic echelons join in a sevenfold paean of praise giving worship to God and to the Lamb. All of creation joins in adoration.

> And every created thing which is in heaven and on the earth and under the earth and on the sea, and all things in them, I heard saying, "To Him who sits

62

on the throne, and to the Lamb, be blessing and honor and glory and dominion forever and ever." And the four living creatures kept saying, "Amen." And the elders fell down and worshipped (Verses 12-14).

Once again this worship equates God the Father and God the Son. As all the created order honors Jesus Christ as God, we must do likewise. We must exalt the Lamb with the four living creatures, the twenty-four elders and all the angels of heaven. We must exult in the sovereign plans and purposes of God with all angels and every created thing. This is our place as we stand on the periphery of heaven.

The Four Horsemen

Revelation 6:1-8

The scenes in God's throne room set the stage. We must now grasp the grand sweep of history controlled by God and set in motion by Jesus Christ. The four horsemen of the apocalypse ride forth to play out this history, God's story.

"Then I saw when the Lamb broke one of the seven seals, and I heard one of the four living creatures saying as with a voice of thunder, 'Come'" (verse 1).

Christ begins to open the book by breaking the series of seven seals which hold it closed. John is in rapt attention and full of amazement. He actually sees the Lamb begin His task of unfolding history. When Christ breaks the first seal, one of the four angelic creatures thunders, "Come." The authorized version reads, "Come up here." The words appear to be directed at John. The better manuscripts simply say, "Come." The exhortation is directed to the first horseman. In response, John exclaims, "I looked, and behold, a white horse, and he who sat on it had a bow; and a crown was given to him, he went out conquering and to conquer" (verse 2).

Although the commentators disagree on who or what this horseman represents, I think he is a symbol of the gospel riding forth to victory. This is not Christ himself but the power of the gospel riding through history. The bow fires gospel arrows into the hearts of men and women subduing them to Christ. The words, "conquering" and "to conquer" mean this rider goes forth being victorious for the purpose of victory. Psalm 45:3-5, a messianic Psalm, gives us a similar picture.

Gird Your sword on Your thigh, O Mighty One,
In Your splendor and Your majesty!
And in Your majesty ride on victoriously,
For the cause of truth and meekness and righteousness;
Let Your right hand teach You awesome things.
Your arrows are sharp;
The peoples fall under You;
Your arrows are in the heart of the King's enemies.

We cannot avoid the similarity. The first force of history with which we reckon is the gospel. The gospel will be victorious.

"When He broke the second seal, I heard the second living creature saying, "Come" (verse 3). A second angel calls an engine of history into action as Christ unfolds the purposes of God. "And another, a red horse, went out; and to him who sat on it, it was granted to take peace from the earth, and that men would slay one another; and a great sword was given to him" (verse 4).

One of the great forces of history is war, physical and spiritual. The former portrays and pictures the latter. The force and power of warfare is at once both a manifestation of the evil one and a judgment of God. God permits Satan to rage.

64

Yet war is a judgment coming from the hand of God. Fallen humanity left to its own devices is bent on self-destruction. The deeds of the flesh are manifest as Paul tells us in Galatians 5:19-21:

> Now the deeds of the flesh are evident, which are: immorality, impurity, sensuality, idolatry, sorcery, enmities, strife, jealousy, outbursts of anger, disputes, dissensions, factions, envying, drunkenness, carousing, and things like these, of which I forewarn you, just as I have forewarned you, that those who practice such things will not inherit the kingdom of God.

Those who will not inherit the kingdom instinctively battle the kingdom. This is God's design. He originally told Satan, "I will put enmity Between you and the woman, And between your seed and her seed; He shall bruise you on the head, And you shall bruise him on the heel" (Genesis 3:15). Conflict on both the physical and spiritual levels is inevitable.

The unavoidable consequence of war is famine, a third force in world history.

> When He broke the third seal, I heard the third living creature saying, "Come." I looked, and behold, a black horse; and he who sat on it had a pair of scales in his hand. And I heard something like a voice in the center of the four living creatures saying, "A quart of wheat for a denarius, and three quarts of barley for a denarius; and do not damage the oil and the wine" (Verses 5-6).

In the picture the horseman has scales with which to measure out food for humankind. The voice of God emanating from the throne directs the horseman. A denarius was a day's wages. The dry measure of wheat was a day's supply. Imagine spending all you have each day for food. The cheaper grain was barley. A laborer could scarcely support his family with this daily supply. Essential oil and wine are not touched.

The deeper famine is that of the Word of God. When men and women are denied the privilege of hearing the Word, eternal death follows. This is a serious judgment of God. While the gospel is going forth in victory, some are providentially denied because of location or spiritual insensitivity. In addition, physical war is a diversionary tactic. It so consumes men and women they hardly have time to contemplate the eternal. This is a warning. The forces of war and famine currently affect our world.

John hears the fourth horseman called to action, Death and Hell.

> When the Lamb broke the fourth seal, I heard the voice of the fourth living creature saying, "Come." I looked, and behold, an ashen horse; and he who sat on it had the name Death; and Hades was following with him. Authority was given to them over a fourth of the earth, to kill with sword and with famine and with pestilence and by the wild beasts of the earth (Verses 7-8).

War often brings famine and death follows closely. This horseman is the color of death. He carries a green pallor. His footman running along side is

Hades. Death and Hades are companions for those who do not know Christ. This is the final Word of God for fallen rebels.

These are the great forces at work in history: the gospel, war, famine, and death. The four horsemen are ever present. As the gospel goes forth, God's enemies arise. God perfects His saints in this crucible. Yet we have assurance. Jesus Christ is the Lord of history. World history is His story. Nothing is out of His sovereign control. All things do work together for good in this history for the perfection of God's people. This means the gospel is and will be victorious.

How Long, O Lord?

Revelation 6:9-17

Gospel proclamation proceeds as designed by God. The enemies of the gospel—war, famine, and death—distract the world from essential spiritual truth. We witness these engines of history today. Ultimately God fuels and directs them. Now we see the response of saints in heaven and of the God of heaven to this warfare directed against the gospel. Christ opens the fifth seal of the book of God's decrees. "When the Lamb broke the fifth seal, I saw underneath the altar the souls of those who had been slain because of the word of God, and because of the testimony which they had maintained" (verse 9).

The altar is the altar of sacrifice. The vision presents a picture of martyrs. Remember, this is a picture of reality, not the reality itself. The word for *witness* in the New Testament is μάρτυς, martus. It is the word standing behind our English word martyr. Here we have a picture of those who *bear witness* to Christ and are under the blood of His sacrifice. They are crucified to the world. I therefore think this picture portrays all saints in heaven. Anyone who names the Name of Christ must count the cost of discipleship.

These glorified saints are praying. "And they cried out with a loud voice, saying, 'How long, O Lord, holy and true, will You refrain from judging and avenging our blood on those who dwell on the earth?'" (verse 10). In the vision, the saints pose a question. How long before the true Sovereign rights the scales of justice? How long before the holy God avenges the cruelty of those who war against the gospel?

There is no unrest in heaven. This is a picture. When the justice of God is meted out, heaven rejoices. When will this be? This is the question of saints on earth. "And there was given to each of them a white robe; and they were told that they should rest for a little while longer, until the number of their fellow servants and their brethren who were to be killed even as they had been, would be completed also" (verse 11).

Glorified saints receive robes of actual righteousness and holiness from God through Christ. The posture of heaven is rest. This is the genius of the Sabbath. It should be a foretaste of the rest of heaven. What is God's posture? "Never take your own revenge, beloved, but leave room for the wrath of God, for it is written, 'Vengeance is Mine, I will repay,' says the Lord" (Romans 12:19).

How long? The answer is simple. Again, I think the vision refers to all glorified saints. Upon what do they wait? When the final member of God's elect comes to glory, final, decisive, inescapable judgment strikes the reprobate. This brings us to the sixth seal of the book of God's sovereign decrees.

I looked when He broke the sixth seal, and there was a great earthquake; and the sun became black as sackcloth made of hair, and the whole moon became like blood; and the stars of the sky fell to the earth, as a fig tree casts its unripe figs when shaken by a great wind. The sky was split apart like a scroll when it is rolled up, and every mountain and island were moved out of their places (Verses 12-14).

We readily leap to the conclusion this vision pictures the final demise of planet earth. Remember, this is a word picture. What does it represent? The picture does represent final judgment *spiritually* but not necessarily temporally.

The language reminds us of Joel 2:28-32. Peter quotes this passage on the Day of Pentecost to explain the pouring out of the Holy Spirit (Acts 2:14-21). The passage also reminds us of Haggai 2:6, as interpreted in Hebrews 12:26-29.

> And His voice shook the earth then, but now He has promised, saying, "Yet once more I will shake not only the earth, but also the heaven." This expression, "Yet once more," denotes the removing of those things which can be shaken, as of created things, so that those things which cannot be shaken may remain. Therefore, since we receive a kingdom which cannot be shaken, let us show gratitude, by which we may offer to God an acceptable service with reverence and awe; for our God is a consuming fire.

God's voice shook the earth at Sinai. God promises another more profound shaking. This shaking separates faith in the temporal from the eternal. When Christ dies and returns to life, the foundations of heaven quake. All is altered. Satan is defeated. The sacrifices and ceremonies of ancient Israel cease. The cataclysm of 70 A.D., when Roman armies destroyed the temple, *confirms* this shaking. The language of Matthew 24 fits our picture. The physical shaking of Jerusalem portends final spiritual shaking of all things.

The Bible has wonderful words for those who trust in the death and resurrection of Christ. Jesus Himself says, "He who hears My word, and believes Him who sent Me, has eternal life, and does not come into judgment, but has passed out of death into life" (John 5:24). Such people enter a kingdom which cannot be shaken.

Christ also warns, "He who believes in Him is not judged; he who does not believe has been judged already" (John 3:18). Those rejecting the gospel are under judgment. They are part of the kingdom which is presently being shaken down and ultimately will be broken.

> Then the kings of the earth and the great men and the commanders and the rich and the strong and every slave and free man hid themselves in the caves and among the rocks of the mountains; and they said to the mountains and to the rocks, "Fall on us and hide us from the presence of Him who sits on the throne, and from the wrath of the Lamb; for the great day of their wrath has come, and who is able to stand?" (Verses 15-17).

There is no escape for the small or the great. There is no hiding place. No one is able to stand before the wrath of the Lamb. When unrepentant sinners enter eternity, their fate is sealed. "It is appointed for men to die once and after this comes judgment" (Hebrews 9:27). Physical death is terrible. Final spiritual death is cataclysmic. It is ultimate judgment.

Christians trust in the God of history knowing there is final rest in heaven and final judgment of all evil.

The Mark of God

Revelation 7:1-8

We've seen the gospel riding forth to victory (Reelvation 6:1-2). Enemies intrude (Revelation 6:3-8). The saints in heaven look for the judgments of God to vindicate the gospel (Revelation 6:9-11). During this inter-advent period, God's judgments are ever present (Revelation 6:12-17). As Paul tells us in Romans 1:18, "The wrath of God is revealed from heaven against all ungodliness and unrighteousness of men." God shook heaven and earth at the first coming of Christ. He shook Israel and destroyed, once for all, the temple and its rituals. This was confirmed in 70 A.D. The destruction of Jerusalem was a picture of the final conflagration and shaking at the final judgment. During this inter-advent period, God leads the church to triumph.

> After this I saw four angels standing at the four corners of the earth, holding back the four winds of the earth, so that no wind would blow on the earth or on the sea or on any tree. And I saw another angel ascending from the rising of the sun, having the seal of the living God; and he cried out with a loud voice to the four angels to whom it was granted to harm the earth and the sea, saying, "Do not harm the earth or the sea or the trees until we have sealed the bond-servants of our God on their foreheads." (Revelation 7:1-3)

John now sees four angels at the four corners of the earth holding back four winds. This is a picture. The earth represents the world in a spiritual sense. The four winds are the winds *of the earth*. That is, they are the false teachings and false doctrines emanating from the camps of the world. Of course these false teachings are propagated by people consumed by the world and opposed to God. Paul urges change and steadfastness. "We are no longer to be children, tossed here and there by waves and carried about by every wind of doctrine, by the trickery of men, by craftiness in deceitful scheming" (Ephesians 4:14). Human wisdom inevitably attempts to deceive, if possible, the very elect of God. "False Christs and false prophets will arise and will show great signs and wonders, so as to mislead, if possible, even the elect" (Matthew 24:24).

However, the four winds are held back. The picture is similar to the binding of Satan portrayed in Revelation 20:2. The four winds are not permitted to harm the earth or sea. The latter represents the sea of worldly people and their tumultuous life. An angel with the seal of God comes from the rising of the sun. Malachi 4:2 promises, "But for you who fear My name, the sun of righteousness will rise with healing in its wings; and you will go forth and skip about like calves from the stall." And 2 Peter 1:19 reminds us, "We have the prophetic word made more sure, to which you do well to pay attention as to a lamp shining in a dark place, until the day dawns and the morning star arises in your hearts."

This is a great message of hope. The winds of evil doctrine cannot consume God's elect people. They must receive the mark and seal of God.

This seal is the Holy Spirit in the life of the believer molding the character. Ephesians 1:13 reminds Christians, "You were sealed in Him [Christ] with the Holy Spirit of promise." Ephesians 4:30 urges, "Do not grieve the Holy Spirit of God, by whom you were sealed for the day of redemption." A seal is a mark. Men and women sealed with the Holy Spirit have the mark of God. It is not physical but spiritual. Others see the mark as they observe the fruit of the Spirit cropping out in our lives.

We rightly understand baptism to be a sign and seal of our inclusion in the covenant of grace. Baptism pictures and symbolizes the work of the Spirit. The baptized person is marked by God, separated from the world.

John tells us more about those receiving the seal of God in verses 4-8:

> And I heard the number of those who were sealed, one hundred and forty-four thousand sealed from every tribe of the sons of Israel: the tribe of Judah, twelve thousand were sealed, from the tribe of Reuben twelve thousand, from the tribe of Gad twelve thousand, the tribe of Asher twelve thousand, from the tribe of Naphtali twelve thousand, from the tribe of Manasseh twelve thousand, the tribe of Simeon twelve thousand, from the tribe of Levi twelve thousand, from the tribe of Issachar twelve thousand, the tribe of Zebulun twelve thousand, from the tribe of Joseph twelve thousand, from the tribe of Benjamin, twelve thousand were sealed.

Numbers in Revelation are symbolic. Ten is a number of fullness. Ten times ten represents completeness. Twelve refers to the church. Revelation 21:9-21 describes the bride of Christ, the New Jerusalem. The city has twelve gates and twelve foundation stones. Each side of the city is twelve thousand stadia. The wall is one hundred and forty-four cubits high. This is a perfect city.

The one hundred and forty-four thousand are a picture of the church militant throughout history. The church is true Israel. "For he is not a Jew who is one outwardly, nor is circumcision that which is outward in the flesh. But he is a Jew who is one inwardly; and circumcision is that which is of the heart, by the Spirit, not by the letter; and his praise is not from men, but from God" (Romans 2:28-29). The text confirms this by placing Judah first in the list of tribes. Reuben was actually the firstborn son of Israel. However, because Christ came from the tribe of Judah, this tribe is listed first among all the tribes, thus signifying the true nature of this list as the church. In addition, Levi was not numbered among the tribes receiving a portion of the promised land. Levi's inheritance was the Lord. The inclusion of Levi indicates this list also refers to spiritual Israel—the church—rather than physical Israel.

This church wages war against the dragon, the beast, the false prophet, and the great harlot. "Our struggle is not against flesh and blood, but against the rulers, against the powers, against the world forces of this darkness, against the spiritual forces of wickedness in the heavenly places" (Ephesians 6:12).

Tribulation and Glory

Revelation 7:9-17

The scene turns to the church triumphant in heaven (Revelation 7:9-12):

> After these things I looked, and behold, a great multitude which no one could count, from every nation and all tribes and peoples and tongues, standing before the throne and before the Lamb, clothed in white robes, and palm branches were in their hands; and they cried out with a loud voice, saying, "Salvation to our God who sits on the throne, and to the Lamb." And all the angels were standing around the throne and around the elders and the four living creatures; and they fell on their faces before the throne and worshipped God, saying, "Amen, blessing and glory and wisdom and thanksgiving and honor and power and might, be to our God forever and ever. Amen."

All heaven rejoices when salvation is applied to God's people and they are marked with the Holy Spirit. In the previous vision we saw one hundred and forty-four thousand. We now see a different picture. No one knows the number of God's elect. "These angels and men, thus predestinated and foreordained, are particularly and unchangeably designed; and their number so certain and definite, that it cannot be either increased or diminished" (Westminster Confession of Faith 3:4). However, God alone counts this multitude. The great Commission is fulfilled. Every tribe, tongue, people, and nation is represented in heaven.

These people are "before the throne and before the Lamb" (verse 9). The first commandment, "You shall have no other gods before Me" (Exodus 20:3), is fulfilled in their lives. They are justified, having received the gift of Christ's righteousness; they are clothed in white robes. They are at peace with God; they have palm branches in their hands.

These saints have one message, "Salvation to our God who sits on the throne, and to the Lamb" (verse 10). Salvation comes from God alone through Jesus Christ. "There is salvation in no one else; for there is no other name under heaven that has been given among men by which we must be saved" (Acts 4:12).

These saints rejoice in the salvation of God. They rejoice to see the advance of the church militant. Jesus puts it this way, "I tell you that in the same way, there will be more joy in heaven over one sinner who repents than over ninety-nine righteous persons who need no repentance" (Luke 15:7).

The angels of heaven add their assent to this cry. Amen, truly, they cry. "Amen, blessing and glory and wisdom and thanksgiving and honor and power and might, be to our God forever and ever. Amen." This is a seven-fold paean of praise similar to the adoration of Revelation 5:13. It is a hymn praising the perfection of God's Salvation through Jesus Christ, a perfect, full, and glorious hymn.

In the vision, one of the twenty-four elders gathered around the throne turns to John to speak to him. Suddenly John finds himself in the midst of the heavenly gathering. He is in intimate conversation with one of the participants. John *is* one of the participants.

> Then one of the elders answered, saying to me, "These who are clothed in the white robes, who are they, and where have they come from?" I said to him, "My lord, you know." And he said to me, "These are the ones who come out of the great tribulation, and they have washed their robes and made them white in the blood of the Lamb (Revelation 7:13-14).

It is important to know who these saints in heaven really are. This seems to be the reason for the question posed to John. John defers to the elder who informs him they are tribulation saints.

Is this *the Great Tribulation* discussed so much by Futurists? I think not. We have a vision before us, a representation of reality but not reality itself.

Jesus warns the church in Thyatira regarding her assent to those who lead astray:

> I have this against you, that you tolerate the woman Jezebel, who calls herself a prophetess, and she teaches and leads My bond-servants astray so that they commit acts of immorality and eat things sacrificed to idols. Behold, I will throw her on a bed of sickness and those who commit adultery with her into *great tribulation*, unless they repent of her deeds (Revelation 2:20-21, italics added).

From the perspective of John, this is present or imminent tribulation not distant or remotely future.

In Matthew 24, Jesus warns us false prophets will attempt to mislead us (verse 11). He tells us we will be delivered to tribulation (verse 9). This, says Jesus, is among other portents, only the beginning (verse 8). Jesus pointedly confirms these words in John 16:33, "In the world you have tribulation, but take courage; I have overcome the world." The world is the place of great tribulation, turmoil, and trouble. Christ also says, "But the one who endures to the end, he will be saved" (Matthew 24:13). We must all persevere under the trial of worldly tribulation. As James exhorts, "Consider it all joy, my brethren, when you encounter various trials, knowing that the testing of your faith produces endurance. And let endurance have its perfect result, so that you may be perfect and complete, lacking in nothing" (James 1:2-4).

The picture John sees is of saints who have gained the victory through perseverance. The elder therefore adds in Revelation 7:15-17:

> For this reason, they are before the throne of God; and they serve Him day and night in His temple; and He who sits on the throne will spread His tabernacle over them. They will hunger no longer, nor thirst anymore; nor will the sun beat down on them, nor any heat; for the Lamb in the center of the throne will be their shepherd, and will guide them to springs of the water of life; and God will wipe every tear from their eyes.

The picture brings us to consummate glory. Compare Revelation 21:4 and 21:6. Glory comes through tribulation. This is the will and the way of God. Compare also Philippians 2:8-9.

The second great section of Revelation, chapters 4-7, closes with scenes of glory. The gospel is going forth. War, famine and death divert energy. Yet the church militant graduates to triumph and glory through perseverance in tribulation.

Prayer and Justice

Revelation 8:1-5

By now you suspect how I am interpreting Revelation. I am not a Futurist. The Futurist says all of Revelation beyond chapter three belongs to the era immediately preceding the second coming of Christ. I am also not taking the preterist position. The preterist insists the bulk of Revelation was fulfilled in the age of the infant church or in close proximity to it. All of the book except the very end is past. A third position, the historical, sees Revelation fulfilled in the early centuries of the Christian era.

Although I have preterist leanings, I am taking a philosophy of history approach to this book. I think it portrays the great forces at work in history under the hand of God. The book is God's story. It is the unfolding of His story issuing in the ultimate victory of Christ, of the gospel, and of God's people. In it we see the majesty of Christ. We are called to do so.

I am also taking the position this book repeatedly rehearses the victory of Christ in the gospel from differing perspectives. In this book we have a set of seven recitations. Such repetition or recapitulation is typical in biblical apocalyptics.

As a novice, I find a handful of books speaking directly to Revelation especially helpful among the many commentaries from differing perspectives I am consulting. These are alphabetically: Patrick Fairbairn, *Prophecy*; Albertus Pieters, *The Lamb, The Woman and the Dragon*; James Ramsey, *Revelation, An Exposition of the First 11 Chapters*; Henry B. Swete, *Commentary on Revelation*; Milton S. Terry, *Biblical Apocalyptics*; and Geoffrey B. Wilson, *Revelation*.

Revelation 8 begins the third part of this great book of visions encompassing chapters 8-11. Six seals of the book of God's decrees have been opened. The seventh releases the seven trumpets. Before the trumpets begin to sound, we see something startling. "When the Lamb broke the seventh seal, there was silence in heaven for about half an hour" (Revelation 8:1).

Here we have a dramatic pause. All heaven is in awe of God, Jesus Christ, the divine purposes unfolding, and the prospect of awesome events to come. The moment of silence, half an hour as compared to eternity, accentuates the drama. It is a time, as Psalm 46:10 exhorts, to "Be still, and know that I [am] God: I will be exalted among the heathen, I will be exalted in the earth." Here, all heaven pauses to contemplate the Almighty. This is a great Selah[51] in the song of heaven.

In the same breath John says, "And I saw the seven angels who stand before God, and seven trumpets were given to them" (Revelation 8:2). The seven

---

[51] Selah may refer to a dramatic pause, crescendo, or musical interlude in the Psalms. See *New American Standard Bible, Reference Edition* (LaHabra: The Lockman Foundation, 1995), 778.

angels who stand before the throne of God receive seven trumpets. The picture is gradually filled with divinely appointed participants in the heavenly drama. We see this even before the seven angels sound their trumpets.

"Another angel came and stood at the altar, holding a golden censer; and much incense was given to him, so that he might add it to the prayers of all the saints on the golden altar which was before the throne" (Revelation 8:3).

The image is actually an angel standing over the altar of incense. This altar is symbolic of prayers ascending before the face of God. The angel adds much incense to the prayers of God's people, an image of the intercession of Christ. We dare not go before God in our own names. Our prayers are feeble, imperfect, mixed with sin. Christ's intercession perfects our prayers and makes them a sweet smelling savor before God. "And the smoke of the incense, with the prayers of the saints, went up before God out of the angel's hand" (Revelation 8:4).

What is the content of these prayers? The next verse gives us a hint. "Then the angel took the censer and filled it with the fire of the altar, and threw it to the earth; and there followed peals of thunder and sounds and flashes of lightning and an earthquake" (Revelation 8:5). The angel throws fire from the altar on the earth. The earth symbolizes the world as a spiritual system opposed to God. The devil is the god of this untoward kingdom (2 Corinthians 4:4). The fire is the fire of judgment. The thunder, lightning, and earthquake represent the judgments of God brought against the earth. Compare just two other texts. "At Thy rebuke they fled; At the sound of Thy thunder they hurried away. The mountains rose; the valleys sank down To the place which Thou didst establish for them" (Psalm 104:7-8). "From the LORD of hosts you will be punished with thunder and earthquake and loud noise, *With* whirlwind and tempest and the flame of a consuming fire" (Isaiah 29:6).

This is the picture. What is the meaning? The interpretation, it seems to me, is quite simple. The prayers of God's people are part of the means used by God to bring about His glorious purposes. We know means are never disconnected from ends. For example, if people are to be converted to faith in Christ, and we know they are, we must proclaim the gospel to the lost. Means and ends are always coupled. "How then will they call on Him in whom they have not believed? How will they believe in Him whom they have not heard? And how will they hear without a preacher?" (Romans 10:14). In this case, the prayers of God's people are part of the means used by God to bring judgment upon evil and evil doers.

We see something similar under the heading of the fifth seal in Revelation 6:9-10:

> When the Lamb broke the fifth seal, I saw underneath the altar the souls of those who had been slain because of the word of God, and because of the testimony which they had maintained; and they cried out with a loud voice, saying, "How long, O Lord, holy and true, will You refrain from judging and avenging our blood on those who dwell on the earth?"

The saints under the altar of burnt offering represent all whose sins are covered by the blood of Christ. In the vision they cry to God in prayer seeking God's justice. They want the scales of justice and righteousness set right.

The application is simple. The prayers of God's people are part of the means used by God to bring about His ends. Part of His will involves the glorious salvation of His people. God also wills the punishment of those who obstinately and maliciously oppose Him and His Christ. Prayer for perfect justice to be meted out is prayer in accordance with God's will. Such prayer ought to be uttered. Such prayer must be voiced. We must pray for the brandishing of the sword of God's judgment. Such prayer will be answered (1 John 5:14-15). The incense rising before God is in part our prayers.

The Trumpets Sound

Revelation 8:6-11

Once the prayers of God's people rise to heaven, warning shots are fired across the bow of 'good' ship earth. Remember, the earth represents the world system opposed to God. Warnings of impending doom *now* resonate through the earth. "And the seven angels who had the seven trumpets prepared themselves to sound them" (Revelation 8:7). Once the stage is set for this act of the drama, the seven angels prepare to sound their warnings.

I say these are warnings of impending doom because the seven trumpets remind us so much of the people of Israel invading Jericho in Joshua 6:6-9:

> Joshua the son of Nun called the priests and said to them, "Take up the ark of the covenant, and let seven priests carry seven trumpets of rams' horns before the ark of the Lord." Then he said to the people, "Go forward, and march around the city, and let the armed men go on before the ark of the Lord." And it was so, that when Joshua had spoken to the people, the seven priests carrying the seven trumpets of rams' horns before the Lord went forward and blew the trumpets; and the ark of the covenant of the Lord followed them. The armed men went before the priests who blew the trumpets, and the rear guard came after the ark, while they continued to blow the trumpets.

As Israel circled Jericho, no one spoke. However, seven priests blew seven trumpets as the people marched around the city once a day for six days. What went through the minds of the people of Jericho? They knew the stories of God's work in redeeming Israel (Joshua 2:8-11). The people of Jericho feared Israel and were fully warned of the impending catastrophe. On the seventh day, the warnings complete, God gave the city to Israel. Joshua 6:15-16 rehearses what took place:

> Then on the seventh day they rose early at the dawning of the day and marched around the city in the same manner seven times; only on that day they marched around the city seven times. At the seventh time, when the priests blew the trumpets, Joshua said to the people, "Shout! For the Lord has given you the city."

We see a parallel when the seventh trumpet sounds in Revelation and the original Hallelujah Chorus is sung. "Then the seventh angel sounded; and there were loud voices in heaven, saying, 'The kingdom of the world has become the kingdom of our Lord and of His Christ; and He will reign forever and ever'" (Revelation 11:15). These words apply to Jericho, to our day, and to the end of the age.

Revelation 8:7: "The first sounded, and there came hail and fire, mixed with blood, and they were thrown to the earth; and a third of the earth was burned up, and a third of the trees were burned up, and all the green grass was burned up."

The trumpet blasts remind us of the plagues sent upon Egypt. Those plagues warned the people and gave them opportunity to repent. The same is true here. Revelation 9:20-21 laments:

> The rest of mankind, who were not killed by these plagues, did not repent of the works of their hands, so as not to worship demons, and the idols of gold and of silver and of brass and of stone and of wood, which can neither see nor hear nor walk; and they did not repent of their murders nor of their sorceries nor of their immorality nor of their thefts.

As for the first plague, once again the earth represents the world as a spiritual entity opposed to God. The trees and grass are the fruit of the world, institutions built on atheistic presuppositions. Such institutions are set on self-destruct. Modern education and social structures built on ungodly principles leave in their wake a host of destroyed lives. Abortion abounds. Suicide is the second highest cause of death among teenagers. This is a clear warning sounded by God unheeded by educators and social engineers.

"The second angel sounded, and something like a great mountain burning with fire was thrown into the sea; and a third of the sea became blood, and a third of the creatures which were in the sea and had life, died; and a third of the ships were destroyed" (Revelation 8:8-9).

Mountains often represent kingdoms and nations in Scripture. The casting of this mountain into the sea may represent the dissolution of governments. They melt into the sea of nations. A wake of dislocation and destruction follows.

Ancient examples abound. The recent disintegration of the USSR seems to me to be a contemporary one. This atheistic power collapsed and much turmoil has followed, physical and spiritual. Unfortunately, many cults have moved in to fill the spiritual void. This too is a warning. Atheistic power, no matter what the form, cannot stand.

> The third angel sounded, and a great star fell from heaven, burning like a torch, and it fell on a third of the rivers and on the springs of waters. The name of the star is called Wormwood; and a third of the waters became wormwood, and many men died from the waters, because they were made bitter (Revelation 8:10-11).

Stars are often messengers of God. In Revelation 1:20, the seven stars are no doubt the pastors of the seven churches. A star which falls is ecclesiastical power on the descent, perhaps teachers of the Word falling from a proper understanding of Scripture. Such persons pervert the Word and lead people astray. The waters of life within the church are embittered. They no longer provide spiritual health and vitality. They lead poor souls to eternal death. Such is the case in our modern world where political correctness supersedes biblical correctness. Falling stars are a warning from God.

A word is in order regarding the figure of one third found in verses 7, 8, and 10. Under the third and fourth seals, the horsemen are given authority over a fourth of the earth. What is the difference under the seven trumpets? As men and women refuse to heed the judgments and warnings of God, He ups the ante. These judgments and warnings become more severe. This is true on both corporate and individual levels. The application of the Word of God is simple. "Therefore repent and return, so that your sins may be wiped away, in order that times of refreshing may come from the presence of the Lord" (Acts 3:19).

A Falling Star

Revelation 8:12-9:1

We continue the exposition of the third major section of Revelation, chapters 8-11, with the fourth trumpet.

"The fourth angel sounded, and a third of the sun and a third of the moon and a third of the stars were struck, so that a third of them would be darkened and the day would not shine for a third of it, and the night in the same way" (Revelation 8:12).

The fourth trumpet affects the lights of heaven. Once again, remember this book is full of symbols. The symbols portray certain realities. For example, physical death is devastating. Scripture often uses physical death to portray the agonies of hell—spiritual death. Similarly, with regard to we humans, light is a symbol for either the rational capabilities given to us by God as part of His image (common grace) or gracious spiritual illumination given by God.

Note John 1:4 and 1:9. "In Him was life, and the life was the Light of men." "There was the true Light which, coming into the world, enlightens every man." Calvin comments:

> I think that this is a reference to that part of life in which men surpass the other animate creatures. It is as if we were saying that the life given to men was not life in general but life united with the light of reason. . . . [B]eams from this light are shed on the whole race of men, as I said before. For we know that men have this unique quality above the other animals, that they are endowed with reason and intelligence and that they bear the distinction between right and wrong engraven in their conscience.[52]

In our day, people use the powers of reason unreasonably. Tragic diseases such as Alzheimer's also dim the powers of reason, intelligence, and conscience.

Jesus warns us, "If anyone walks in the night, he stumbles, because the light is not in him" (John 11:10). He adds to this in the Sermon on the Mount, "If your eye is bad, your whole body will be full of darkness. If then the light that is in you is darkness, how great is the darkness" (Matthew 6:23).

Spiritual blindness is more devastating than physical blindness. It leads to eternal death. When God withdraws the light of heaven, men and women lose their sensibilities. Rationality goes out the window. Spiritual illumination is also wanting. This is the picture the fourth warning trumpet gives us. Surely the warning applies to our day as it applied in the first century. Once again, because God is *warning* the earth, there is a limit set on the plague. Without repentance, more serious calamity is inevitable.

"Then I looked, and I heard an eagle flying in midheaven, saying with a loud voice, 'Woe, woe, woe to those who dwell on the earth, because of the

---

[52] John Calvin, *The Gospel According to St. John*, 1-10, Trans. T. H. L. Parker (Grand Rapids: Eerdmans, 1959), 11, 15.

remaining blasts of the trumpet of the three angels who are about to sound'" (Revelation 8:13).

Yes, the first four trumpets are only the beginning. An angel in midheaven, one having a message in full view, although often unseen, pronounces a three-fold woe. In Hebrew this represents the superlative. When Isaiah saw the Lord in the temple, the seraphim "called out to another and said, 'Holy, Holy, Holy, is the Lord of hosts, The whole earth is full of His glory'" (Isaiah 6:3). God is the holiest of all. Here, the three-fold woe represents the gravest of warnings given by God to rebel humankind. As in the case of the seven seals, the trumpets are divided into a set of four and a set of three.

Revelation 9:1-11 gives us the vision of the fifth trumpet. We will deal with this in two parts, the opening of the abyss (verses 1-6) and the description of the locusts (verses 7-11). Revelation 9:1 states "Then the fifth angel sounded, and I saw a star from heaven which had fallen to the earth; and the key of the bottomless pit was given to him." This is a fascinating picture. We see a star which has fallen from heaven. This is heavenly power now groveling in the earth, the spiritual world opposed to God. This power is identified in verse 11 "as the angel of the abyss; his name in Hebrew is Abaddon, and in the Greek he has the name Apollyon." This angel is the Destroyer. The commentators generally accept he is Satan. They refer to Isaiah 14:13 where the king of Babylon (verse 4) haughtily affirms, "I will ascend to heaven; I will raise my throne above the stars of God, and I will sit on the mount of assembly in the recesses of the north." He is a type or picture of the rebellion of the devil. Isaiah 14:12 says of him, "How you have fallen from heaven, O star of the morning, son of the dawn! You have been cut down to the earth, you who have weakened the nations!" Jesus says of this angel of light, "I was watching Satan fall from heaven like lightning."

The picture gives us a star falling from heaven, the angel of the abyss. The reality involves emissaries of the devil arising from within the pale of the visible church proclaiming doctrines of demons. These are teachers and pastors, filled with the spirit of the world and full of themselves, spewing pious sounding worldly wisdom in the name of the Christ. Paul warns the Ephesian elders, "I know that after my departure savage wolves will come in among you, not sparing the flock; and from among your own selves men will arise, speaking perverse things, to draw away the disciples after them" (Acts 20:29-30). He also tells Timothy to beware. "The Spirit explicitly says that in later times some will fall away from the faith, paying attention to deceitful spirits and doctrines of demons (1 Timothy 4:1).

The key to the bottomless pit, the abyss, is given to this angel. In other words, ministers and teachers who oppose Christ have the keys of hell. Jesus promised Peter, "I will give you the keys of the kingdom of heaven" (Matthew 16:19). Through the apostles, the officers of the church are charged with the duty of receiving people in the visible church and excluding others. In part, teaching and ruling elders do this through teaching. Emissaries of the abyss also open that awful place to poor souls through their false teachings.

82

The First Woe, Smoke from the Abyss

Revelation 9:2-11

The angel of the abyss uses the key given to him. "He opened the bottomless pit, and smoke went up out of the pit, like the smoke of a great furnace; and the sun and the air were darkened by the smoke of the pit" (Revelation 9:2). Literally, the angel opened the shaft of the abyss. The abyss is the home of demons (Luke 8:31), the home of the beast (Revelation 11:7), and the dragon's prison (Revelation 20:1). The picture is of a long shaft reaching into the pit of hell.

Smoke billows from the pit like a great blast furnace from which belch seemingly uncontainable heat and smoke. The smoke fills the air and conceals the sun. This is the picture. The doctrines of hell often conceal the light of heaven. Men and women choke on the pollution coming from hell. Eternal life is threatened.

The picture becomes more complex, perplexing, and awesome. "Then out of the smoke came locusts upon the earth, and power was given them, as the scorpions of the earth have power" (verse 3). The locust plague from hell reminds us of the plague which threatened Egypt. Then the locust brought physical devastation. These locusts bring spiritual woe. The earth is that spiritual kingdom ruled by the devil. The spiritual plagues fall on this kingdom.

The locusts are given specific directions. "They were told not to hurt the grass of the earth, nor any green thing, nor any tree, but only the men who do not have the seal of God on their foreheads" (verse 4). The targets of the plagues coming from hell are people not having the seal of God, the Holy Spirit. The grass and trees are fruits of the earth, the institutions of the world built on anti-Christian principles. We will speak more about them under the heading of the beast and false prophet. The institutions of government, education, science, and the arts are used to propagate anti-Christian views and remain active. Those who act within them to propagandize the earth find woe.

There are limits placed on the locusts. "And they were not permitted to kill anyone, but to torment for five months; and their torment was like the torment of a scorpion when it stings a man. And in those days men will seek death and will not find it; they will long to die, and death flees from them" (verses 5 and 6).

Remember, the vision is symbolic. It pictures reality but is not reality itself. The locust are demon spirits loosed from hell propagating their lies through human instruments. They do not have the prerogative of bringing eternal death to their victims. The ferocity of these plagues increases as men and women ignore them and think they can work through them. What is the purpose of the plagues? Revelation 9:20 gives us a hint: "The rest of mankind, who were not killed by these plagues, did not repent of the works of their hands, so as not to worship demons, and the idols of gold and of silver and of brass and of stone and of wood."

The scorpion sting is sharp, very painful, and potentially deadly. Here the pain is spiritual. It is pain of heart, soul, and conscience. It is so severe men and women do almost anything to escape but are unable. Suicide is the second highest reason for death among teens. The only remedy for fallen sin-filled souls is Jesus Christ. Otherwise torment increases exponentially and eternally.

The torment is also limited to a span of five months. All the numbers in Revelation are symbolic. Five is less than seven, the number of completeness. The torments of soul do not issue in repentance. These agonies of spirit are incomplete without repentance. Those who are under these plagues of spirit are like governor Felix in Acts 24:25 when Paul spoke to him. "As he was discussing righteousness, self-control and the judgment to come, Felix became frightened and said, 'Go away for the present, and when I find time I will summon you.'" Conviction is not full blown. It does not produce repentance. This is a warning of immense significance. The object of the trumpet plagues is repentance. Without repentance, eternal death is the result.

Verses 9-11 describe the locusts:

> The appearance of the locusts was like horses prepared for battle; and on their heads appeared to be crowns like gold, and their faces were like the faces of men. They had hair like the hair of women, and their teeth were like the teeth of lions. They had breastplates like breastplates of iron; and the sound of their wings was like the sound of chariots, of many horses rushing to battle. They have tails like scorpions, and stings; and in their tails is their power to hurt men for five months. They have as king over them, the angel of the abyss; his name in Hebrew is Abaddon, and in the Greek he has the name Apollyon.

Keep in mind the symbols picture reality. The reality is how powerful, stately, and enticing the doctrines of hell can be. The locusts are like powerful horses ready for battle. They have crowns. They are stately rulers in their domain and are to be respected. So the purveyors of falsehood in our worldly institutions present themselves.

These horses have human faces. They are not brute beasts but articulate and attractive teachers. At the same time, these children of the devil and these broods of vipers are enticing and vicious. The hair of women is their crown. They are beautiful to look upon. Beauty is often deceptive. The teeth of lions bring to mind 1 Peter 5:8: "Your adversary, the devil, prowls around like a roaring lion, seeking someone to devour." This is how the devil operates. He seeks to kill and destroy. The warning goes unheeded.

The breastplates of iron may portray the fact these devilish teachers and preachers think their positions are impenetrable. They are stout of heart and proud. They think they will be victorious. Their teachings set forth an intimidating sound. This is true in religion, education, science, and the arts. The Kantian critique dominates religious discussion. Evolution is taught as fact. Atheistic thought is supremely unscientific in its rejection of the Creator. Movies, television, and the theater major in promoting perversity and mocking holiness. Yet the sophisticated voice of the expert intimidates and frightens. We have already spoken of the scorpion sting, the five months of verse 10 and of Abaddon and Apollyon of verse 11.[53]

[53] See Pages 83 and 82 respectively.

The Second Woe, Two Hellish Armies

Revelation 9:12-21

"The first woe is past; behold, two woes are still coming after these things" (Revelation 9:12). These woes are warnings of the last three trumpets. They exhort the earth to repent. Unheeded, they lead to the seven vials in which God's judgment is spent. These warnings can come to us at any time as individuals or to the institutions we hold dear.

"Then the sixth angel sounded, and I heard a voice from the four horns of the golden altar which is before God, one saying to the sixth angel who had the trumpet, 'Release the four angels who are bound at the great river Euphrates'" (verses 13-14).

The sounding of trumpet number six reveals a golden altar. It is the altar of burnt offering under which we saw the saints killed because of the testimony they maintained (Revelation 6:9). God answers the prayers of these saints (Revelation 6:10). We see a similar representation in Revelation 8:3-5. The voice from the altar, symbolic of God answering prayer, commands the release of four angels bound at the Euphrates.

These are no doubt evil angels. The word translated *bound* is the word used in Revelation 20:2 where Satan is bound. The concepts appear to be the same. There is also a parallel here with the four winds held back until the sealing of God's bond-servants (Revelation 7:1-3).

The Euphrates was the eastern extremity of the Israelite kingdom, the ancient visible church of God. The enemies of Israel traditionally came from the east. God warns Israel through Isaiah, "In that day the Lord will shave with a razor, hired from regions beyond the Euphrates (that is, with the king of Assyria), the head and the hair of the legs; and it will also remove the beard" (Isaiah 7:20). The picture is of an attack on the visible kingdom of God. Remember, this kingdom was and is a mixed multitude. Enemies abound within the pale of the church. Their existence is a warning call of God. See my understanding of the fifth trumpet given in the preceding sections. The attack viewed under the sixth trumpet is also a warning call to repentance. I keep repeating this because of the overall importance to our discussion and application.

"And the four angels, who had been prepared for the hour and day and month and year, were released, so that they would kill a third of mankind" (verse 15). The emphasis here is on the eternal decrees of God. He determines all that transpires. Christ is in the process of opening the book of God's plans. He is setting the purposes of God in motion. There is always a good reason in the good plan of the good God for the seeming evil which befalls so many. As said above, the good purpose here is a call to repentance.

Under the fifth trumpet, the restraint on the locust was "they were not permitted to kill anyone" (verse 5). When warnings are unheeded and sorrow is worldly in nature (2 Corinthians 7:10), repentance does not follow. Death is inevitable. This fixes responsibility. Under the sixth trumpet, the warning is more severe. The angels released from the east may kill a third of mankind. Under the seven seals, the judgments and warnings are limited to one fourth of the earth (Revelation 6:8). As people in this life see and experience war, famine and death, both physical and spiritual, and fail to see the hand of God behind the forces at work, the terror of the warnings escalates. Fear is indeed a component of conviction (Acts 24:25). And a fear of the Lord is but the beginning of a wise understanding of reality (Proverbs 1:7, 9:10). Now the limits of power born by the four angels is withdrawn slightly. We see a similar picture in the plagues brought on Egypt and also in the wonderful Book of Job.

"The number of the armies of the horsemen was two hundred million; I heard the number of them" (verse 17). Again, the numbers in Revelation are symbolic. Literally, the number is two myriads of myriads. The angels gathered around the throne in worship and adoration number myriads of myriads (Revelation 5:11). In this chapter we see two hellish armies under the fifth and sixth trumpets. Satan's ploys are in two primary areas, the forces of political power and of worldly wisdom. We see this graphically in the emergence of the beast and false prophet (Revelation 13). Although the forces of the enemy are formidable and we must not underestimate them, they are limited and doomed.

And this is how I saw in the vision the horses and those who sat on them: the riders had breastplates the color of fire and of hyacinth and of brimstone; and the heads of the horses are like the heads of lions; and out of their mouths proceed fire and smoke and brimstone. A third of mankind was killed by these three plagues, by the fire and the smoke and the brimstone which proceeded out of their mouths. For the power of the horses is in their mouths and in their tails; for their tails are like serpents and have heads, and with them they do harm (Verses 17-19).

Once again, the vision describes the enemy army. We see the pride of the horsemen in their brightly colored breastplates. They are bright blue and orange and red representing the smoke and brimstone and fire coming from hell. The horses are lion-like, ferocious. The battle they wage is a verbal one. They spew the deception and lies of hell as they belch fire, smoke, and brimstone. Those who swallow their lies are rewarded with the same fire, smoke, and brimstone. Note the power of the horses is in their mouths and in their tails. They have tails like serpents. The good reason behind the plagues is fulfilled. Those heeding the warnings of God repent. Those who do not are confirmed as reprobate. God's awesome purposes stand.

The rest of mankind, who were not killed by these plagues, did not repent of the works of their hands, so as not to worship demons, and the idols of gold and of silver and of brass and of stone and of wood, which can neither see nor hear nor walk; and they did not repent of their murders nor of their sorceries nor of their immorality nor of their thefts (verses 20-21).

Jesus says it all, "You serpents, you brood of vipers, how will you escape the sentence of hell? (Matthew 23:33).

The Trumpet Calls Practically Applied

Let's reflect on what we have seen. My refrain with regard to the seven trumpets reminds us these blasts from heaven are warnings from God. They call the earth, the spiritual system opposed to God, to repent. The trumpets are also warning calls to the visible church. Enemies exist within and without. Repentance should be a way of life. The world enters the heart and core of the church. Worldly rather than biblical standards set the tone and content of her worship.

Under the heading of the six trumpets we see the warnings escalate. We see hearts become hard like that of Pharaoh. As mentioned in the previous section, these warning trumpets sound all around us in varying degrees. From a contemporary perspective, what are these warning blasts from heaven?

Over a period of decades, interesting phenomena have been occurring in our culture. We have been moving into what many philosophers and theologians call the post-modern era. Along with the devolution of the moral base undergirding education, science, and the arts, we see scientists, educators, and entertainers whose endeavors depend upon the rational use of rationality, leap into the irrational. At the same time, anti-Christian governmental power, executive, legislative, and judicial, is seriously challenging cultural foundations.

My position is the beast of Revelation 13:1 is anti-Christian governmental power having atheistic roots and exercised in and through kingdoms and nations. The false prophet of Revelation 13:11 and 16:13 is the power of hell manifested in the fields of education, science, and the arts and exercised through atheistic based institutions such as schools, laboratories, and studios. These are the twin armies of political power and worldly wisdom represented in Revelation 9.

These engines of evil work to produce virulent opposition to God and the rule of Christ over all areas of life. When the lights of heaven are dimmed by smoke from the pit, these powers are at work. They are warning trumpets of God.

Not too many years ago the Supreme Court banned the display of the Ten Commandments in public school classrooms. This was a symptom of a greater problem. Moral relativism was and is pervading our culture. Along with it came many unfortunate and unseemly teachings. The battles are verbal ones. As the vision tells us, "For the power of the horses is in their mouths and in their tails; for their tails are like serpents and have heads, and with them they do harm" (Revelation 9:19).

This power is exhibited in counter productive sex education which touts the use of condoms rather than abstinence. The DARE program exhibits this power and has done little if anything to reduce drug use among teens. Death education is another avenue of this unseemly hellish voice. It tells teens the last and final way for them to take charge is suicide. This contributes to suicide being the second largest cause of death among teens. Not only so, it claims many poor souls for hell. Situation ethics once taught in our high schools under the rubric of Values Clarification has devolved into more pervasive moral relativism and political correctness. Evolution is taught as fact rather than a theory. Pluralism, egalitarianism, and multiculturalism rule. Christianity is much too narrow to tolerate. The self esteem movement is losing steam because it has resulted in lowering educational standards and increasing violence with its me-first approach.

The outcropping of these teachings—making the work of the church difficult at best—is a series of trumpet blasts from God. He warns us to see how counter productive these materialistic, hedonistic, and atheistic approaches to life really are. Worldly wisdom is waging war against our souls. Are we listening? Is the world listening?

On the other side of the coin we see struggles with anti-Christian civil government erupt in violence. I recall driving through the south from my home in New Jersey to Fort Hood, Texas. It was 1964. I had a little red Volkswagen beetle with a New Jersey license plate on the back. I drove through small towns where the streets were lined with police and National Guardsmen fully equipped with weapons and riot control gear. This frightened me. The civil rights movement was in full bloom.

I was in Pasadena, California, attending seminary when serious racial riots erupted. You could drive on the freeway through Watts in central Los Angeles and see the city burning. You could see riflemen in the streets who were later awarded combat ribbons for their service during that terrible time. There was a machine gun emplacement under the shadow of the seminary's main entrance. This was frightening.

Twenty years later a similar riot broke out in Los Angeles. This demonstration occurred in response to the police beating of one Rodney King and the subsequent verdict. The O.J. Simpson trial had policemen on alert. One of the attorneys for Mr. Simpson challenged the jury to right the wrongs of racial injustice and send a message to the police by setting the defendant free. A direct challenge to the legal system of America.

At the other end of the spectrum we have a similar rebellion against governmental powers, the rise of militia groups and paramilitary cultic societies. Over the years we have witnessed the domestic tragedies of Ruby Ridge, Waco, the Oklahoma City bombing, and the Freemen of Montana. Internationally and more recently, we have seen the rise of anti-Christian Muslim fanaticism epitomized in the destruction of the twin towers of the World Trade Center on September 11, 2001. These unseemly forces arising are trumpets sounded from heaven warning the earth, the church, and anti-Christian powers, to repent. The anguish provoked by these events is immense.

There were debates in Christian circles over the Oklahoma City bombing. Was this event a judgment of God or an act of the devil? The debate raged back and forth. My response was and is simply, Yes. I think of the seven trumpets. As earlier trumpets go unheeded, more devastating warning calls to repent have been seen and will be seen. These are trumpet sounds, sent in God's providence, calling us to repentance. Are we listening? Is the world listening? Revelation 9:20 warns, "The rest of mankind, who were not killed by these plagues, did not repent of the works of their hands, so as not to worship demons, and the idols of gold and of silver and of brass and of stone and of wood, which can neither see nor hear nor walk."

From all of this you once again note I am taking a philosophy of history approach in interpreting the book of Revelation. Revelation 10 shows us that we find the proper answer to God's judgments and call to repent in the Bible and in the Christian gospel.

[The more recent warning trumpets of God include involvement in the Iraq and Afghanistan wars. Many souls perished in these wars and many men and women lost arms and legs and were severely wounded emotionally. Hurricane Katrina ravaged the gulf coast. Terrorism again came close to home in the Boston bombing. Northern Africa has once again been in chaos. Severe winter storms caused havoc in 2014. God's warning trumpets are sounding all around us. God calls us to repent of our evil ways and turn back to Him. Is the world listening? Are we listening?]

The Bitter-Sweet Gospel

Revelation 10:1-11

Revelation more or less reviews the present age seven times. The first section, chapters 1-3, is firmly rooted in the first century history with letters to seven representative churches. In section two, chapters 4-7, we saw the throne of God, the Lion of the tribe of Judah and Lamb that was slain yet lives, and His opening of the great scroll with seven seals. We are presently viewing the third section, chapters 8-11. Chapter 10 answers the warning blasts of the trumpets. Six trumpets have sounded. The warnings of God mount. Trumpet seven is yet to come. In the interim, John says, "I saw another strong angel coming down out of heaven, clothed with a cloud; and the rainbow was upon his head, and his face was like the sun, and his feet like pillars of fire" (Revelation 10:1).

This messenger looks much like the Son of Man. Compare Revelation 1:13-15. However, Revelation does not portray Christ as an angel. This is a messenger of Christ, a strong angel. Another strong angel sought someone to open the book of seven seals (Revelation 5:2). A strong angel will also execute God's judgment against Babylon (Revelation 18:21). The rainbow reminds us of God's covenant not to ever again destroy the earth with a flood (Genesis 9:11). This angel is a messenger bearing the good news of God's covenant.

"And he had in his hand a little book which was open. He placed his right foot on the sea and his left on the land" (verse 2). This little book contrasts with the great book of chapter 5. The former is the book of God's decrees. The little book is the Word of God, specifically the gospel. This little book reminds us of Ezekiel 2:8-3:3, where God gives the prophet a scroll to eat and tells Ezekiel to prophesy. We therefore take this little book to be the Word of God. This little book is open. The gospel is available to all who will listen. God's decrees are hidden.

That the angel stands on the land and on the sea indicates both his stature and his authority. He is a mighty, a strong angel. His authority is pervasive, covering all the earth. The gospel goes forth to every tribe, tongue, people, and nation.

"And he cried out with a loud voice, as when a lion roars; and when he had cried out, the seven peals of thunder uttered their voices" (verse 3). The loud voice accentuates the authority of the angel. The voice is a voice of a lion, The Lion of the Tribe of Judah. This is the message of Jesus Christ. The angel represents Christ and the gospel of Christ. Immediately, thunder rumbles. There is clarity in revelation and there is obscurity. When the elect hear the voice of The Lion through His representatives, they hear the Word of God. It is quite the opposite for those outside of Christ as indicated in verse 4.

"When the seven peals of thunder had spoken, I was about to write; and I heard a voice from heaven saying, 'Seal up the things which the seven peals of thunder have spoken and do not write them.'"

Some men and women hear the Word clearly. To others it is just noise. John understood the seven peals of thunder as perhaps the perfect judgments of God. The reprobate fail to properly understand the Word of God, the thunder from heaven. When Jesus was close to His death He cried to God, "'Father, glorify Your name.' Then a voice came out of heaven: 'I have both glorified it, and will glorify it again'" (John 12:28). How did the multitudes perceive the voice of the Father? "So the crowd of people who stood by and heard it were saying that it had thundered" (John 12:29). They hear the sound but they do not recognize the voice of God. The company of Paul experienced a similar thing on the road to Damascus. "The men who traveled with him stood speechless, hearing the voice [*sound*, NASV margin] but seeing no one" (Acts 9:7). Paul explains in Acts 22:9, "And those who were with me saw the light, to be sure, but did not understand the voice of the One who was speaking to me." This is the meaning of verse 4. God discloses the things of salvation to some and hides them from others. Jesus gives thanks for this. "I praise You, Father, Lord of heaven and earth, that You have hidden these things from the wise and intelligent and have revealed them to infants" (Matthew 11:25).

> Then the angel whom I saw standing on the sea and on the land lifted up his right hand to heaven, and swore by Him who lives forever and ever, who created heaven and the things in it, and the earth and the things in it, and the sea and the things in it, that there will be delay no longer, but in the days of the voice of the seventh angel, when he is about to sound, then the mystery of God is finished, as He preached to His servants, the prophets (Revelation 10: 5-7).

There is no real delay in working out the purposes of God. The gospel in all its glory is going forth and covering the earth. The judgments of God are coming to completion. The seventh trumpet will sound. Before this, time will be filled with the events determined before the foundation of the world. When these events unfold, the mysteries of God are revealed. These mysteries are now locked in the words of the prophets.

What must John do? Verses 8-10:

> Then the voice which I heard from heaven, I heard again speaking with me, and saying, "Go, take the book which is open in the hand of the angel who stands on the sea and on the land." So I went to the angel, telling him to give me the little book. And he said to me, "Take it and eat it; it will make your stomach bitter, but in your mouth it will be sweet as honey." I took the little book out of the angel's hand and ate it, and in my mouth it was sweet as honey; and when I had eaten it, my stomach was made bitter.

First, John must ingest the Word of God. It must become His life. This Word of the gospel is sweet. It is a Word bringing life. The Word of the gospel can also be very bitter. It spells eternal judgment for those who reject the Savior.

Second, John must preach the message of sweetness, the life of the gospel, and the message of bitterness, life without the Christ of the gospel. God also

93

charges us with nothing less. "And they said to me, 'You must prophesy again concerning many peoples and nations and tongues and kings'" (verse 11).

Images of the Church

Revelation 11:1-8

After John's commission to preach the bitter-sweet gospel, and ours, we have two visions of the church. "Then there was given me a measuring rod like a staff; and someone said, 'Get up and measure the temple of God and the altar, and those who worship in it'" (Revelation 11:1).

The temple is the church. We are dealing with symbols. The symbol portrays the reality. The temple is a regular picture and type of the church (Ephesians 2:20-22 and 1 Peter 2:4-5). John is given a measuring rod with which to inspect the integrity of the temple. The standard given to us with which to measure the church, and those in it, is the Bible, the Word of God. This is our inerrant *rule* for faith and life. Who gave the measuring rod to John and who gave the directions is not said. We have no difficulty inferring this is divine command.

Verse 2: "Leave out the court which is outside the temple and do not measure it, for it has been given to the nations; and they will tread under foot the holy city for forty-two months." The court outside the temple is the court of the Gentiles. This was, during the time of Jesus, Paul, and John, the court into which Gentiles might enter. Beyond this point they could go only on pain of death. This outer court and the inner court taken together were the visible temple of God. This is the picture.

It tells us the church of Christ is a mixed multitude. Within the pale of the church reside those who have been born again. There are also those who only profess Christ outwardly or who are antagonistic to Christ yet align themselves with a Christian church.

Those who are born again take the rule of God's word seriously and measure their lives by it. Those who are not born again pay lip service to the Word. Within they are hostile. We *see* only the outside of the temple. We *know* it contains two courts. We cannot readily distinguish between these two courts in this life. The vision reveals the problem. Jesus expounds the same truth in the parable of the wheat and the tares in Matthew 13:24-30.

We have a second image of the church beginning in verses 3-4. "And I will grant authority to my two witnesses, and they will prophesy for twelve hundred and sixty days, clothed in sackcloth. These are the two olive trees and the two lampstands that stand before the Lord of the earth." The text takes us to Zechariah 4:11-14:

> Then I said to him, "What are these two olive trees on the right of the lampstand and on its left?" And I answered the second time and said to him, "What are the two olive branches which are beside the two golden pipes, which empty the golden oil from themselves?" So he answered me, saying, "Do you not know what these are?" And I said, "No, my lord." Then he said, "These are the two anointed ones who are standing by the Lord of the whole earth."

The scene is the rebuilding of the temple after the Babylonian captivity. Zerubbalel, the governor of Judah, and Joshua, the high priest, led the way. God anointed them to rebuild His temple. They accomplished their work by the power of the Spirit (Zechariah 4:6, Haggai 2:4). This vision pictures the work of the church.

Our text images the witnessing church. Why two witnesses? "By the mouth of two or three witnesses every fact may be confirmed" (Matthew 18:16). In this context, Jesus makes a startling revelation about Himself and His disciples. About himself: "While I am in the world, I am the Light of the world" (John 9:5). What happens when He leaves this earth? Jesus says to us: "You are the light of the world" (Matthew 5:14). The *witnessing* church, powered by the Spirit, is the light of the world. This church will encounter persecution.

Verses 5-6 portray persecution:

> And if anyone wants to harm them, fire flows out of their mouth and devours their enemies; so if anyone wants to harm them, he must be killed in this way. These have the power to shut up the sky, so that rain will not fall during the days of their prophesying; and they have power over the waters to turn them into blood, and to strike the earth with every plague, as often as they desire.

Those who turn against the witnessing church feel the heat of the Word of judgment. When views of perdition fail to warn and heaven fails to woo, there is eternal death. There is a sense in which the power of life and the sentence of judgment are in the hands of the church. This is truly awesome. Compare Psalm 149:5-9

> Let the godly ones exult in glory;
> Let them sing for joy on their beds.
> *Let* the high praises of God *be* in their mouth,
> And a two-edged sword in their hand,
> To execute vengeance on the nations,
> And punishment on the peoples;
> To bind their kings with chains,
> And their nobles with fetters of iron;
> To execute on them the judgment written;
> This is an honor for all His godly ones.
> Praise the LORD!

And hear the words of Jesus: "I will give you the keys of the kingdom of heaven; and whatever you bind on earth shall have been bound in heaven, and whatever you loose on earth shall have been loosed in heaven" (Matthew 16:19).

Only in God's time does the testimony of the church wane. Verses 7-8: "When they have finished their testimony, the beast that comes up out of the abyss will make war with them, and overcome them and kill them. And their dead bodies will lie in the street of the great city which mystically is called Sodom and Egypt, where also their Lord was crucified." Seeming death comes. Revival follows. Pentecost followed the rejection of the long expected Messiah.

The Reformation followed the Dark Ages. The Great Awakening threw light on an enlightened but darkened age. We live in new dark ages. Yet the witnessing church cannot be extinguished. Revival is inevitable.

Verse 7 portends Armageddon. See Revelation 16:1-16. The spirit of Babylon, the great city (Revelation 17:18), sometimes manifested in Sodom and Egypt, is doomed. Jerusalem of old succumbed to the spirit of Babylon. The modern church surely also has done so. The heirs of the Calvinistic congregationalism in New England ordain homosexuals. Presbyterians are leaning in the same direction. This is death in the broad church, the outer court of the Gentiles. The remnant, the inner court, the church supplied by the Spirit, remains. The beast from the abyss cannot extinguish the true witness of Christ in the church.

For an explanation of the forty-two months and twelve hundred and sixty days, see comments on Revelation 12:14.

Images of the World

Revelation 11:9-14

The Word of God, the gospel, is the only answer to the warning trumpets of God to repent (Revelation 10). We must repent and believe the gospel. The church proclaims the gospel and is measured by the gospel (Revelation 11:1-8). Now we clearly see the reaction of the world to the church and to the proclamation of the Word of God. The broad church, the outer court of the temple, "dies." When the church seems to perish, when the witness of the church becomes dim, the world rejoices. "Those from the peoples and tribes and tongues and nations will look at their dead bodies for three and a half days, and will not permit their dead bodies to be laid in a tomb" (verse 9).

Those from the peoples, tribes, tongues, and nations are representatives of the unbelieving world. It is the dead bodies of the two witnesses which are exposed for three and one half days. The witness of the church appears dead. Yet the true temple of God lives.

That these people do not allow the bodies to be buried indicates their brutality and vile hatred of the church. However, the three and one half days reminds us of Lazarus. When Jesus approached the tomb, John 11:39 relates, "Jesus said, 'Remove the stone.' Martha, the sister of the deceased, said to Him, 'Lord, by this time there will be a stench, for he has been dead four days.'" The three and one half days in Revelation 11:9 indicates the two witnesses do not cause the stench expected by those who hate them.

Verse 10: "And those who dwell on the earth will rejoice over them and celebrate; and they will send gifts to one another, because these two prophets tormented those who dwell on the earth." The earth represents the *world*, that spiritual system led by Satan and opposed to Christ. When the witness of the church falls silent, the world cheers. The torment to those who dwell on the earth is a torment of conscience. When the church is silent, the conscience of the world is not a bother.

Revival comes to the church through the Spirit of God. Verse 11: "But after the three and a half days, the breath of life from God came into them, and they stood on their feet; and great fear fell upon those who were watching them." The days of relative weakness in witness pass. They are short. New life enters the church. The dry bones rattle and rise from the dust of the grave. The Puritans, especially, believed in and prayed for times of revival. When death seemed to overtake the church, they sought God for refreshment from on high. We too need similar times of awakening and revival.

One of the evidences of spiritual awakening is fear. Individuals come to see their eternal peril because of sin. They grasp the reality of hell as a just payment for their sins. They dread the judgment of God. Their only recourse is to seek His face for mercy in forgiveness.

This fear promotes a seeking after God. It is, to be sure, a seeking based upon self interest. The desire is the preservation of life. In this context, what do we do with Romans 3:11? "There is none who understands, there is none who seeks for God." The standard approach is that no person seeks God if not born again. Is this true? My response is that no person seeks God if not impelled to do so by God. External pressure may be exerted in many ways to constrain persons to seek God. This is the burden of Psalm 83:13-16. Here is a prayer crying to God to bring the fear of God upon sinners.

O my God, make them like the whirling dust,
Like chaff before the wind.
Like fire that burns the forest
And like a flame that sets the mountains on fire,
So pursue them with Your tempest
And terrify them with Your storm.
Fill their faces with dishonor,
That they may seek Your name, O Lord (italics added).

God's whole purpose in warning sinners is that they would repent. Here God uses His power to order creation to bring fear to the hearts of sinners and constrain them to seek His face. They would naturally not do this. Fear instilled by God is designed to constrain them to seek Him.

This is actually merciful and gracious of God. Were God to withdraw even His common grace, sinners would have no qualms of conscience regarding their lives or eternity. The application of common grace in engendering fear is an act of mercy.

Verse 12 continues: "And they heard a loud voice from heaven saying to them, 'Come up here.' Then they went up into heaven in the cloud, and their enemies watched them." Remember, this is a vision symbolizing truth. In the vision there is ascension from earth to heaven. This is a picture of Colossians 1:13. "He [God] rescued us from the domain of darkness, and transferred us to the kingdom of His beloved Son." The visible church rises to new life. People change before a watching world. This, too, engenders fear in the heart of people who know they need to be different or else they are doomed.

The voice calling forth new life is that of God. God brings about this new life in a sovereign way as He causes people to seek His face. They seek God by placing themselves under the hearing of His Word. This brings them in contact with the means of salvation, the means of grace. "For you have been born again not of seed which is perishable but imperishable, that is, through the living and enduring word of God" (1 Peter 1:23).

In the interim, a watching world must brace for judgment. "And in that hour there was a great earthquake, and a tenth of the city fell; seven thousand people were killed in the earthquake, and the rest were terrified and gave glory to the God of heaven" (verse 13). The city is likely Jerusalem, earlier referred to as Sodom and Egypt (verse 8), a microcosm of unbelief. Compare Isaiah 1:10 where Isaiah calls Jerusalem and its inhabitants Sodom and Gomorrah. "Hear the word of the LORD, You rulers of Sodom; Give ear to the instruction of our God, You people of Gomorrah." Jerusalem now represents the Christ-rejecting world.

When the sixth trumpet sounds its warning (Revelation 9:13-15), the world floods the church. This is an earthquake. God extracts His tithe. The seven thousand refers to spiritual death coming to those doomed to that state (1 Peter 2:8). This, too, is a cause for fear. It is a call to repentance (Revelation 9:20-21). Some give glory to God out of hearts filled with love for Him. Others give Him glory from perdition. "The second woe is past; behold, the third woe is coming quickly" (verse 14).

The Hallelujah Chorus

Revelation 11:15-19

We now conclude the third section of Revelation, chapters 8-11. The sixth warning trumpet sounded (Revelation 9:13), the second woe is past and the third woe is coming upon those who refuse to repent and turn in faith to Christ as Lord and Savior. As in previous cases, the third woe and the seventh trumpet are synonymous. Revelation 11:15: "Then the seventh angel sounded; and there were loud voices in heaven, saying, 'The kingdom of the world has become the kingdom of our Lord and of His Christ; and He will reign forever and ever.'"

This powerful text stands behind "The Hallelujah Chorus" in Handel's *Messiah*. The choir here involves all those gathered around the throne of God. There are the four living creatures, the twenty-four elders, myriads of angels, and a multitude of glorified saints.

The domain of the devil is no longer the world. The gospel's victory is complete. The first horseman of the four horseman of the apocalypse has completed his task. "He went out conquering to conquer" (Revelation 6:2). Christ reigns. This is the announcement at the end of the age.

Verse 16 begins the response to this grand declaration. "And the twenty-four elders, who sit on their thrones before God, fell on their faces and worshipped God." Why worship God? His plans and purposes are brought to consummation. The song of the elders begins in verse 17: "We give You thanks, O Lord God, the Almighty, who are and who were, because You have taken Your great power and have begun to reign." God, not the universe, is eternal. God, not man, is almighty. He is the ruler of the universe. In what sense does God *begin His reign* at the consummation? At present, Christ reigns as mediator. He is bringing all His and our enemies under the sway of His power. "Then comes the end, when He hands over the kingdom to the God and Father, when He has abolished all rule and all authority and power" (1 Corinthians 15:24). First Corinthians 15:28 then says, "When all things are subjected to Him, then the Son Himself also will be subjected to the One who subjected all things to Him, so that God may be all in all." God is to be and will be all in all.

The song continues: "And the nations were enraged, and Your wrath came, and the time came for the dead to be judged, and the time to reward Your bond-servants the prophets and the saints and those who fear Your name, the small and the great, and to destroy those who destroy the earth" (verse 18).

In the end, God will balance the scales of justice. Let the nations rage. God laughs. See Psalm 2:1-4. The nations are the unbelieving world. God's wrath justly punishes their rebellion, sin, idolatry, fornication, adultery, homosexuality, thievery, etc., etc., etc.

The dead are the dead in sin, the dead spiritually. They receive wrath, justly. The bond-servants of God love Christ. "The fear of the Lord is the beginning of knowledge" (Proverbs 1:7). "The fear of the Lord is the beginning of wisdom" (Problems 9:10). God brings such fear *upon* unbelievers in His providential dealings with them. Many reject this fear. Some grasp it and seek God's face. This is common grace. Special grace, applied to the elect, brings reverence before God and Christ into the hearts of the elect.

The earth is the sphere of the devil. It is composed of people ruled by that spiritual kingdom. They oppose God. Those who destroy the earth are leaders who degrade Christ and direct men and women away from Christ. Such men and women find they have heaped up wrath for the day of wrath. "Because of your stubbornness and unrepentant heart you are storing up wrath for yourself in the day of wrath and revelation of the righteous judgment of God" (Romans 2:5). In the song of the elders, that day has come. The elders give thanks for the awesome and awful judgments of God.

The scene shifts to the inner precincts of heaven in verse 19. "And the temple of God which is in heaven was opened; and the ark of His covenant appeared in His temple, and there were flashes of lightning and sounds and peals of thunder and an earthquake and a great hailstorm."

The temple we now see is the prototype. "For Christ did not enter a holy place made with hands, a mere copy of the true one, but into heaven itself" (Hebrews 9:24). The earthly temple was a type and picture of the heavenly. The true temple is in heaven. When the veil of the earthly temple was torn from top to bottom, this indicated Christ opened the true temple in heaven. Those who trust in the sacrifice of Christ as the only adequate payment for their sins have access into God's throne room.

There we find the ark of the covenant. In this box we see "a golden jar holding the manna, and Aaron's rod which budded, and the tables of the covenant" (Hebrews 9:4). Each of these items reminds us of sin and blessing. The manna reminds us of how God's people often grumble about God's provision. It also symbolizes the life of Christ. He is the true bread which came down from heaven (John 6:33). Aaron's rod reminds us of how God's people often grumble against their leaders. It also reminds us God is the one who sovereignly chooses us and our leaders (Numbers 17:5). The tablets of stone were those tablets upon which God Himself inscribed the Ten Commandments with His own finger (Exodus 31:18, Deuteronomy 9:10). The Ten Commandments remind us of our sins against God and the righteousness of Christ imputed to us by faith. We receive bread from heaven; God has chosen us; the righteousness of Christ is imputed to us. This is our access into the inner sanctuary of God. Hallelujah!

The flashes of lightning, thunder and hail are a salute to the power of God. The images point to the judgments of God. Viewed from within the sanctuary this is a display of "the solemn salvos, so to speak, of the artillery of heaven, with which each series of visions is concluded" (Alford). All heaven salutes the Sovereign God and worships His Majesty. Thus Revelation once again brings us to the end of time. We review the same terrain again in Revelation 12-14 from different perspectives.

The Woman and the Dragon

Part One

Revelation 12:1-5

Chapters 12 through 14 compose the fourth section of this great book. It is the center section of the seven. It begins with visions concerning the revelation and coming of Jesus Christ. Revelation 12 exalts Christ and exults in His coming. We begin with verses 1-2. "A great sign appeared in heaven: a woman clothed with the sun, and the moon under her feet, and on her head a crown of twelve stars; and she was with child; and she cried out, being in labor and in pain to give birth."

The sign or portent which John sees is in heaven, not simply in the sky but in heaven itself. The veil is drawn back and we are given heavenly perspective. To be sure, we are dealing with the highly symbolical. We do not see reality. We see that which portrays reality.

Here is a woman. She represents the church in all ages, both militant and triumphant. She is both ancient Israel and the New Testament church. She is Israel come into her own. This woman is clothed with the sun. She has the resplendent glory of Christ, the imputed righteousness of the "sun of righteousness" (Malachi 4:2). This is a heavenly view of the church. From our earthbound perspective the church lacks luster. She is divided and blemished. Yet, according to Christ, she is "the light of the world" (Matthew 5:14).

From the world's perspective, the church is of little consequence. From God's perspective, the church is all glorious. She has "the moon under her feet." In God's eyes, the church is of intense significance. She has an exalted position. She also has "a crown of twelve stars." In chapter one, stars are the angels of the seven churches, the messengers or ministers of God. Here, perhaps, we see the apostles as the crown of the church. We follow their teachings in Scripture.

The woman is in travail. Ancient Israel was in great travail awaiting the Messiah. Christ would come and deliver Israel from earthly bondage and establish His kingdom. Surely this is a portrayal of the coming of Christ and the suffering of Israel as she is brought to the "fullness of time" (Galatians 4:4).

Revelation 12:3-4 continues.

> Then another sign appeared in heaven: and behold, a great red dragon having seven heads and ten horns, and on his heads were seven diadems. And his tail swept away a third of the stars of heaven and threw them to the earth. And the dragon stood before the woman who was about to give birth, so that when she gave birth he might devour her child.

We see another sign, a great red dragon. He is identified for us. He is "the serpent of old who is called the devil and Satan" (verse 9). He is red signifying his rage and anger. He has seven heads. The number seven refers to completeness or perfection. The dragon has complete sway in his domain which is the world. By world I mean the spiritual kingdom of darkness which is opposed to God.

The dragon has ten horns. The horn represents power. There are more horns than heads. We often say people are educated beyond their intelligence. In this case, I cannot help but think the ten horns show us the power of the dragon outruns his wisdom. The dragon is described as having seven crowns. As mentioned, his power is complete within his own domain. Men and women are "slaves of sin" (Romans 6:20) and "through fear of death" are "subject to slavery all their lives" (Hebrews 2:15). Christ must deliver His people from this slavery (Matthew 1:21). He therefore came into the world "that through death He might render powerless him who had the power of death, that is, the devil" (Hebrews 2:14). As I John 3:8 says, "The Son of God appeared for this purpose, to destroy the works of the devil."

Using his great power, Satan "swept away a third of the stars of heaven." Again this is a picture of reality, not reality itself. If the stars are the messengers of God, pastors of churches, as in Revelation 1:20, Satan uses the sting of his tail to deceive a large percentage of ministers and bring about their fall. We must not underestimate the cunning of the devil.

The residents of hell know the Bible far better than many Christians. The significance of the first gospel promise was not lost on Satan. "And I will put enmity between you and the woman, and between your seed and her seed; He shall bruise you on the head, and you shall bruise him on the heel" (Genesis 3:15). This diabolical Adversary therefore stalks the woman. We see the history of Israel in the background. Satan stands before the woman like Dr. Death hoping for an abortion. He is also ready to strangle a live born child. Herod's plots to search out Christ and kill Him in Bethlehem loom large in our thinking.

Verse 5, "And she gave birth to a son, a male child who is to rule all the nations with a rod of iron; and her child was caught up to God and to His throne." Christ is born. Emphasis is upon the fact the child is male. Let there be no mistake. This is a portrayal of Genesis 3:15. Verse 5 reminds us of Psalm 2:7-9 and God's promise to His Son.

> I will surely tell of the decree of the Lord:
> He said to Me, "You are My Son,
> Today I have begotten You.
> Ask of Me, and I will surely give the nations as Your inheritance,
> And the very ends of the earth as Your possession.
> You shall break them with a rod of iron,
> You shall shatter them like earthenware.

The rod of iron may represent the scepter of a strong and mighty King. Christ is the Lion of Judah. God promised, "The scepter shall not depart from Judah, nor the ruler's staff from between his feet" (Genesis 49:10). Christ was born a King (Matthew 2:2). For this reason, the vision passes immediately to Christ's victory over darkness, His ascension and Session on the throne of God.

Here is another of the many places in Revelation where the deity of Christ is fully presented. Jesus Christ entered heaven where "He must reign until He has put all His enemies under His feet. The last enemy that will be abolished is death" (1 Corinthians 15:25-26). Christ therefore presently sits on the throne of God. With the angels we sing, "Glory to God in the highest" (Luke 2:14).

The Woman and the Dragon

Part Two

Revelation 12:6-12

We continue our commentary with Revelation 12:6. "Then the woman fled into the wilderness where she had a place prepared by God, so that there she would be nourished for one thousand two hundred and sixty days." When the male child is exalted to heaven out of the reach of the dragon, the woman flees to the wilderness. We are reminded of Israel's wilderness sojourn and the care of God during those years. Israel's wilderness experience pictured the church in the world (1 Corinthians 10:6 and 11).[54] We are now in the wilderness of the world looking forward to crossing the verge of Jordan and entering the promised land of heaven. As the woman is nourished by God in the wilderness, so God cares for His church.

A specific time frame is mentioned, twelve hundred and sixty days. This is matched by the period given to the two witnesses to prophesy in Revelation 11:3. It is a three and a half year period in which the beast is given authority in Revelation 13:5. The parallel is Daniel 7:25 where we are told a king "will speak out against the Most High and wear down the saints of the Highest One, and he will intend to make alterations in times and in law; and they will be given into his hand for a time, times, and half a time." Historically, Antiochus Epiphanes desecrated the temple in Jerusalem and brought suffering upon the Jews from the middle of 168 to the end of 165 BC.

Even though the three and a half year period calls Antiochus to mind, in our vision, we do not take the numbers literally but symbolically. We have a short period of intense persecution. God cares for His church in times of weal and times of woe. This seems to be the lesson.

"And there was war in heaven, Michael and his angels waging war with the dragon. The dragon and his angels waged war, and they were not strong enough, and there was no longer a place found for them in heaven" (Revelation 12:7-8).

Here we must really appreciate the imagery presented. The vision presents, symbols representing reality. To understand the significance of this we need only ask a simple question. Can there be war in heaven with all of its attendant hatred, disquietude and upheaval? The answer is no. Literal war is impossible in God's heaven. The deeds of the flesh recorded in Galatians 5:19-21 have no place in heaven. Such things are excluded. What then does this text picture?

We have a further visual portrayal of Genesis 3:15, "I will put enmity between you and the woman, and between your seed and her seed." Michael is

---

[54] In 1 Corinthians 10:11, Paul reminds us, "these things happened to them as an example," literally, τυπικῶς or typically.

106

the prince of Israel (Daniel 10:21). His aid is promised when God's people face distress (Daniel 12:1). Daniel 10:13 indicates Persia also had a spiritual power, a prince, standing behind it. In other words, while spiritual powers, good and evil, are in conflict, the actual battles rage between people unified by darkness on one side and light on the other. Paul rightly analyzes the situation saying, "Our struggle is not against flesh and blood, but against the rulers, against the powers, against the world forces of this darkness, against the spiritual forces of wickedness in the heavenly places" (Ephesians 6:12).

The war is on earth and it is real. It is portrayed as being in heaven. This was important to understand for Christians who were on the front lines of battle in the first century. It is important to realize for those of us on the front lines of battle with the world today. More importantly we ask, Who has the victory? "And the great dragon was thrown down, the serpent of old who is called the devil and Satan, who deceives the whole world; he was thrown down to the earth, and his angels were thrown down with him" (Revelation 12:9). Satan and all his minions are defeated. The reference to being thrown down on the earth is a pictorial way of relating total conquest. Earlier we saw the dragon sweep a third of the stars from heaven and throw them to the earth. This was the deception and demise of messengers, ministers, of God. Similarly, the devil is defeated. He too is thrown to the earth.

When did this dramatic defeat occur? Colossians 2:15 directs us by speaking of Christ. "When He had disarmed the rulers and authorities, He made a public display of them, having triumphed over them through it [*the cross*, NASB margin]. At this point in history, Satan was disarmed and defeated. Hence we hear the victor's song in verses 10-11.

> Then I heard a loud voice in heaven, saying, "Now the salvation, and the power, and the kingdom of our God and the authority of His Christ have come, for the accuser of our brethren has been thrown down, he who accuses them before our God day and night. And they overcame him because of the blood of the Lamb and because of the word of their testimony, and they did not love their life even when faced with death."

Notice the victors are now those who trust in the sacrifice of Christ and pledge allegiance to Him. They may not win every battle, but they win the war. The song continues with an exhortation. "For this reason, rejoice, O heavens and you who dwell in them. Woe to the earth and the sea, because the devil has come down to you, having great wrath, knowing that he has only a short time (verse 12).

In Revelation, the earth and the sea represent the spiritual world of darkness and the teaming "sea" of unbelievers. This is why the beast rises from the sea (Revelation 13:1). Heaven rejoices over the victory of the Lamb.

The angels of God were longing to see these things (1 Peter 1:12). How could the righteous God pass over the sins previously committed by Old Testament saints and justly allow them in heaven (Romans 3:25)? The answer was now coming to light. Christ entered the world as a babe in Bethlehem. He lived a perfect life and died a perfect death on behalf of sinners. Through Christ, God could "be just and the justifier of the one who has faith in Jesus" (Romans 3:26). God's people could be justly forgiven because of Christ and clothed with righteousness of Christ. Once again we sing with the angels, "Glory to God in the highest" (Luke 2:14).

The Woman and the Dragon

Part Three

Revelation 12:13-17

Jesus Christ came into the world, lived a perfect life, died on behalf of undeserving sinners, rose again from the dead, ascended into heaven, took His place on the throne of God, and rules as King of kings and Lord of Lords. In all of this, Christ plundered the devil's domain and took a host of captives for His own kingdom. This defeat of the devil is symbolized in Revelation by his being cast down to the earth. The earth in Revelation represents the domain of Satan. Theologically, it is the world and all that is opposed to God. Revelation 12:13 goes on to say, "And when the dragon saw that he was thrown down to the earth, he persecuted the woman who gave birth to the male child."

In defeat, the devil turns in rage against the church of God. This is the story of the church throughout the present age. Persecution waxes strong and then wanes. When persecution comes, the church flourishes. God always protects and sustains His people. "But the two wings of the great eagle were given to the woman, so that she could fly into the wilderness to her place, where she was nourished for a time and times and half a time, from the presence of the serpent" (Revelation 12:14).

The place of safety for the people of God is under His mighty wings. Psalm 17:8 pleads, "Keep me as the apple of the eye; Hide me in the shadow of Your wings." And Psalm 91:4 promises, "He will cover you with His pinions, and under His wings you may seek refuge; His faithfulness is a shield and bulwark." Christ uses the same imagery when He laments the unfaithfulness of Israel. "Jerusalem, Jerusalem, who kills the prophets and stones those who are sent to her! How often I wanted to gather your children together, the way a hen gathers her chicks under her wings, and you were unwilling" (Matthew 23:37). So the church is protected and nourished by the Father.

This protection and nourishment persists throughout the present age. The time frame given in verse 14 is taken from Daniel 7:25, "a time and times and half a time." It is the same period mentioned in verse 6 as "one thousand two hundred and sixty days." This is also the period during which the two witnesses of Revelation 11:3 prophesy. In Revelation 11:2 this period is given as forty-two months, the time of the trampling of the holy city. Finally, this is the period of the ascendancy of the beast in Revelation 13.

We do not take these numbers literally but symbolically. The number of days means the days of wilderness wondering for the church are numbered. The forty-two months refer to the relative shortness of the time of our wilderness wandering. The three and one-half years also refer to the relative shortness of this time. This is one-half of seven. The persecution of the church does not come to completion. The church remains. Calamity is cut off suddenly by the return of Christ. The dragon knows his time is short, verse 12.

Satan therefore doubles his efforts. "And the serpent poured water like a river out of his mouth after the woman, so that he might cause her to be swept away with the flood" (Revelation 12:15). The flood of water is a torrent of false doctrine and heresy with which Satan inundates the earth. These are the teachings of the cults which undermine the deity of Christ. They are the teachings of false religion like Islam. They are the false evolutionary suppositions of science. They are the false teachings of philosophy espousing the ultimate goodness of human nature and the ultimacy of the human will.

To too large an extent, these anti-biblical teachings flood the church. Help comes from a strange source. "But the earth helped the woman, and the earth opened its mouth and drank up the river which the dragon poured out of his mouth" (Revelation 12:16). As already stated, the earth represents the world, not physically but spiritually. The world is the domain of Satan, the kingdom of darkness. The world is always ready to swallow the lies of the devil and drink deeply from the fountains of heresy and unbelief.

When the world imbibes, this should be a red flag for the church. She is warned not to drink too deeply of the things of this world and become intoxicated. Unfortunately, the church has drunk deeply at the springs of psychology, management, and entertainment. Rather than being brokers of truth, seminaries are teaching young pastors to major in management, cling to counseling techniques, and learn to entertain their constituents. This is how you build a successful church, by the world's standards. This is the flood coming from the mouth of the dragon.

The final verse in Revelation 12 once again sets before us a vision of Genesis 3:15. God said to the serpent in Eden, "And I will put enmity between you and the woman, and between your seed and her seed; he shall bruise you on the head, and you shall bruise him on the heel." Revelation 12:17 describes the perverse hostility of the dragon. "So the dragon was enraged with the woman, and went off to make war with the rest of her children, who keep the commandments of God and hold to the testimony of Jesus."

I say this is perverse hostility because of the way the vision portrays it. The earth helped the woman. Who then suffers under the wrath of the dragon? It should logically be the earth. This is not so. The dragon makes war with the children of the woman. Satan's hostility and animosity toward the church is completely illogical and irrational.

The children of the woman (Revelation 12:17) or the seed of the woman (Genesis 3:15) are those "who keep the commandments of God and hold to the testimony of Jesus." They love Christ and display this love through obedience. The testimony of Jesus is the gospel of Christ proclaimed by the church. The measure of this gospel is the Word of God (Revelation 11:1). Those "who keep the commandments of God and hold to the testimony of Jesus" persevere to the end. They are "sealed with the Holy Spirit of promise" (Ephesians 1:13). They are recipients of the gospel riding forth to victory (Revelation 6:1-2). They sing with the angels, "Glory to God in the highest" (Luke 2:14).

110

The Beast

Revelation 13:1-10

Once again, Chapters 12 through 14 compose the fourth section of this great book. Revelation 12 reveals the birth of Christ. With Him comes salvation. Revelation 12 also introduces Christ's arch enemy, the dragon. We see the church under siege and under the protection of God. There is titanic spiritual struggle. The two sides of this struggle are expounded in chapters 13 and 14. We see the negative side in chapter 13 with the introduction of two other formal enemies, the beast and the false prophet. We glimpse the positive side with its victory in chapter 14.

We begin with the dragon who makes war with the seed of the woman. "And the dragon stood on the sand of the seashore. Then I saw a beast coming up out of the sea, having ten horns and seven heads, and on his horns were ten diadems, and on his heads were blasphemous names" (verse 1).

Having raged after the woman in the wilderness, the dragon now stands by the sea. This is the sea of humanity outside of Christ. The dragon, Satan, appears to call forth a beast out of the sea. Beasts of this sort represent political and governmental power manifested in worldly kingdoms. The four beasts of Daniel 7 are kingdoms and political powers. This beast bears the image of the dragon having seven heads and ten horns. The ten horns and ten diadems indicate the pervasive power of this beast among the kingdoms of men. The seven heads represent the wisdom of the beast. Jesus told His disciples, "Be shrewd as serpents and innocent as doves" (Matthew 10:16).

Verse 2 describes this beast further. "And the beast which I saw was like a leopard, and his feet were like those of a bear, and his mouth like the mouth of a lion. And the dragon gave him his power and his throne and great authority."

This beast is sly and cunning like a leopard. He has the strength of a bear and is ferocious like a lion. People bow before his roar. When government power speaks, men and women tremble. The devil is also wise. He knows the Bible and theology better than most. He is cunning and deceptive. He imparts his skill to the beast. We have seen many anti-Christian governmental powers arise in the world. The Babylonian and Greek empires were examples. Rome was another. We can mention Hitler's regime and the atheistic power of the USSR. We also add the deteriorating situation in both Canada and the USA. A college professor visiting from the Ukraine during 1993 challenged our congregation with words similar to these, "Seventy years of atheism in the Soviet Union proved unworkable, why are you moving in the same direction?" Excellent question. More recently, we see Islamic leaders exercise religious power for political ends and world dominance. There is no difference between church and state. The beast is active.

Verse 3: "I saw one of his heads as if it had been slain, and his fatal wound was healed. And the whole earth was amazed and followed after the beast." This is a parody, an imitation of Christ. Government views itself as a savior. It has a messianic complex. This is certainly true in the rise of Islam. It is also true in atheistic world systems. Men and women of the earth stand amazed at the power and wisdom of the beast. The earth is the kingdom of darkness, the domain of the devil. The beast, anti-Christian governmental power, is viewed as the earth's messiah. The people of this kingdom willingly follow the beast. They fight for greater governmental power. Sound familiar?

Verse 4: "They worshipped the dragon because he gave his authority to the beast; and they worshipped the beast, saying, 'Who is like the beast, and who is able to wage war with him?'"

The perverted authority behind all anti-Christian governmental power is the devil. We must remember this. Oddly enough, it does not matter whether you are a Republican, Democrat, or Independent. Government is not the answer to any national, moral, medical, or economic problems. God is the one to whom we should turn. However, the power of government is revered by many. Since this is the case, verses 5-7 say:

> There was given to him a mouth speaking arrogant words and blasphemies, and authority to act for forty-two months was given to him. And he opened his mouth in blasphemies against God, to blaspheme His name and His tabernacle, that is those who dwell in heaven. It was also given to him to make war with the saints and to overcome them, and authority over every tribe and people and tongue and nation was given to him.

Because anti-Christian government is obsessed with its own power to save, it mounts various assaults on the church and the God of the Bible.

The forty-two months is the same period the woman, the church, is nourished by God in the wilderness (Revelation 12:6). The days of our wilderness wanderings in this world are numbered (Psalm 90:12, 139:16). This period in which God nourishes the church in the wilderness is also "a time and times and half a time" or three and one half years (Revelation 12:14). This time will be cut off suddenly. The power of the beast, ungodly governmental power, is seen to be dominant only *for a time*.

This is the picture. The result is plain, verse 8: "All who dwell on the earth will worship him, everyone whose name has not been written from the foundation of the world in the book of life of the Lamb who has been slain." People from every tribe, tongue, and nation serve the beast, anti-Christian ungodly government power. Once again, the earth in Revelation is the spiritual world opposed to God. It is composed of the reprobate. They do not have their names in the book of life nor has Christ died for them.

Verses 9-10 warn and encourage. "If anyone has an ear, let him hear. If anyone is destined for captivity, to captivity he goes; if anyone kills with the sword, with the sword he must be killed. Here is the perseverance and the faith of the saints." We must hear the Word of God. First, we will not escape predestined struggle. Second, God's judgments will be executed. Our posture is clear. We must trust God's plans. We must also persevere. We must remember we are privileged to be part of the purposes of God.

The False Prophet

Revelation 13:11-18

"Then I saw another beast coming up out of the earth; and he had two horns like a lamb and he spoke as a dragon" (Revelation 13:11). This second beast, arising from the earth, is always associated with the dragon and the first beast. This second beast *is* the false prophet. Compare Revelation 16:13.

He is lamb-like in appearance. He seems quiet, gentle, harmless and helpful as he delivers his propaganda. Yet he is as dangerous as the dragon. How so? His teachings lead men and women, young people, and children away from Christ. He is anti-Christian power found in education, science, and the arts. Education, science, and the arts were intended by God for building a culture and society obedient to Him. Most colleges and universities were begun by Christians. Modern science got its start with the work of Christian men like Kepler and Pasteur. Formerly, the most cultured art was tied to Scripture whether we speak of music, painting, sculpture, or architecture.

Secular education opposes God, denying any need to acknowledge Him in the classroom, making the work of the church exceedingly difficult at best. Secular science is atheistic at base. It sees no need for God nor does it desire God. Those who acknowledge God and pursue science are castigated as supremely unscientific. Christian theists find it difficult to pursue advanced degrees in science if they are outspoken about God. Secular art not only propagates atheism but it supports amoral and aberrant behavior calling it normal. It paints a caricature of Christianity misrepresenting it as extremist. Homosexuality is acceptable. Exclusive heterosexual monogamy is bigotry.

On the other hand, anti-Christian religions propagate their views and build their cultures using education, science, the media, and the arts. Radical Islam is again a prime example. Muslim radicals indoctrinate the young with a viral hatred for all that is Christian.

What of this second beast? "He exercises all the authority of the first beast in his presence. And he makes the earth and those who dwell in it to worship the first beast, whose fatal wound was healed" (verse 12).

The first beast, ungodly and anti-Christian governmental power, derives its authority from the dragon and delegates authority to educational, scientific, and cultural institutions such as schools, laboratories, museums, and libraries. In our society, such institutions are closely allied to government or government owned and sanctioned. The false prophet leads people in following the beast. After all, government is our messiah.

The actions of the false prophet seem to warrant our devotion. "He performs great signs, so that he even makes fire come down out of heaven to the earth in the presence of men" (verse 13). The works of ungodly education, science, and the arts seem miraculous. Lives are changed through good schooling. Advances in science, space exploration, and medicine for example, are astounding. Explorations of virtual realities via computer boggle our minds.

Special effects in films and on television captivate us. These phenomena seem almost divine in origin. This is the problem. Appearances are deceiving.

The false prophet leads many astray by leading them away from God. "And he deceives those who dwell on the earth because of the signs which it was given him to perform in the presence of the beast, telling those who dwell on the earth to make an image to the beast who had the wound of the sword and has come to life" (verse 14).

Those who dwell on the earth are those opposed to Christ. They are deceived. The wonders performed by the false prophet captivate them. Men and women are to build a culture and society to the glory of God. They are to use government, education, science, and the arts as tools to glorify God. Apostasy is the contrary. Schools, scientific enterprises, and theaters are built to glorify man. Thus the anti-Christian posture of the devil is imaged in the world. Men and women worship the false Christ of government at the behest of ungodly educators, scientists, and artists.

The false prophet breathes life into the institutions built on ungodly principles. "And it was given to him to give breath to the image of the beast, so that the image of the beast would even speak and cause as many as do not worship the image of the beast to be killed" (verse 15). This breath is the life of the dragon, the devil, who seeks the spiritual demise of his victims. In ancient Rome, worship of Caesar became mandatory. Death was the penalty for calling upon Christ as Lord. Such a confession was high treason. In today's culture, those who are not politically correct can suffer serious political and economic sanctions.

The false prophet is ruthless. "And he causes all, the small and the great, and the rich and the poor, and the free men and the slaves, to be given a mark on their right hand or on their forehead" (verse 16). All social and economic categories follow the teachings of the false prophet. They are marked people. The mark of God is the Holy Spirit. Christians have this mark. "You were sealed in Him [Christ] with the Holy Spirit of promise" (Ephesians 1:13). "Do not grieve the Holy Spirit of God, by whom you were sealed for the day of redemption (Ephesians 4:30). When the fruit of the Spirit is manifest in a person's life, we clearly see the mark of the Spirit. Similarly, the mark of the beast is the presence of the unholy spirit. He displays himself in the deeds of the flesh. The mark is on their hand and forehead to indicate all they think and do is guided by the devil.

Those involved with devilish schemes form circles of friendship and fellowship. Today we see unions, political parties, and social organizations of many sorts. They often involve economic and social privileges. This is one way the false prophet propagandizes the earth. Verse 17 says, "And he provides that no one will be able to buy or to sell, except the one who has the mark, either the name of the beast or the number of his name." Here we meet the infamous number of the beast. Verse 18: "Here is wisdom. Let him who has understanding calculate the number of the beast, for the number is that of a man; and his number is six hundred and sixty-six." This number refers to the false trinity composed of the dragon, beast, and false prophet. This number is 666, a number relating to the exaltation of man who desires to make a name for himself (Genesis 11:4). If a number were assigned to the true Trinity it would be 777.

Perfect Victory

Revelation 14:1-10

Part One

Chapter 13 introduced us to the beast, the false prophet, and their work. Now we have a view of the church and her victory through Christ. It is a perfect victory from God's perspective. It is a sevenfold victory. We see the first part of this victory in this section.

"Then I looked, and behold, the Lamb was standing on Mount Zion, and with Him one hundred and forty-four thousand, having His name and the name of His Father written on their foreheads" (verse 1).

We first met the 144,000 in chapter seven. These are the church of God in all ages. Twelve is the number of the church. Compare Revelation 21. One thousand is ten cubed, ten times ten, a number of perfection from the human perspective. A vast number. These are on Mount Zion, another symbol of the church. They also have the mark of God. The Name of God and the Name of the Lamb represent the character of God and of Christ. The church bears the Name and character of God. In this text, I think we have a representation of the church militant. Compare Revelation 7:1-8 and 9-17.[55]

This church has a great work to do. Verse 2: "And I heard a voice from heaven, like the sound of many waters and like the sound of loud thunder, and the voice which I heard was like the sound of harpists playing on their harps." Although on earth, this church has a song from heaven. It is a powerful song. Anyone who has been next to the river at Niagara and has heard the waters rushing toward and over the falls knows in part what this vision portrays. The voice thundered judgment. The voice also sounded the melody of grace. It was the voice of a choir energized by heaven. "And they sang a new song before the throne and before the four living creatures and the elders; and no one could learn the song except the one hundred and forty-four thousand who had been purchased from the earth" (verse 3).

In the vision, the 144,000 are people purchased from the domain of the devil, the earth. They are before the throne of God and the company of angels assembled around that throne. We are those people gathered in worship. We are delegates of heaven laboring in this world. When we assemble for worship we are on the edge of heaven.

This is a new song in that it comes from hearts made new by the Spirit. It is an old song in that it is the old song of redemption. It is at one and the same time, "the song of Moses, the bond-servant of God, and the song of the Lamb" (Revelation 15:3).

The vision describes this worshipping church. Verses 4-5:

---

[55] See Page 70ff.

These are the ones who have not been defiled with women, for they have kept themselves chaste. These are the ones who follow the Lamb wherever He goes. These have been purchased from among men as first fruits to God and to the Lamb. And no lie was found in their mouth; they are blameless.

To be undefiled means chaste with regard to spiritual matters. Adultery is a symbol of idolatry throughout Scripture. Following the Lamb indicates devotion to Him. The first fruits are the part of the harvest belonging to God. This church is full of truth and the Spirit of truth.

We now begin to see the sevenfold victory of the church. We see seven angels, messengers. First, Christ commissions her to preach the everlasting gospel to all creation. Verse 6: "And I saw another angel flying in midheaven, having an eternal gospel to preach to those who live on the earth, and to every nation and tribe and tongue and people." This angel is at the highest point of heaven. He is very visible and unavoidable. The message he brings goes to every tribe, tongue, people and nation. Note this message is directed to those who live on the earth. The earth refers to the world, the domain of Satan. The message is directed at extracting people from his clutches.

We must remember the eternal gospel has two sides. We must also remember, "The fear of the Lord is the beginning of knowledge" (Proverbs 1:7). "The fear of the Lord is the beginning of wisdom" (Proverbs 9:10). Those who rightly fear God experience the salvation of God. Wisdom is therefore not only fearing the wrath of God for sin, wisdom is trusting Christ to take the awful wrath of God for your sin. Wisdom is coming to God through Jesus Christ. Wisdom is glorifying God as the Creator, Redeemer, and Sustainer of life. Here is victory. Look at the message of the angel. Verse 7: "And he said with a loud voice, 'Fear God, and give Him glory, because the hour of His judgment has come; worship Him who made the heaven and the earth and sea and springs of waters.'"

The second part of this announcement of victory involves the fall of evil. "And another angel, a second one, followed, saying, 'Fallen, fallen is Babylon the great, she who has made all the nations drink of the wine of the passion of her immorality'" (verse 8). We meet Babylon. This is a fourth enemy of the cross. The others are the dragon, the beast, and the false prophet. Babylon is the capital of evil epitomized in that ancient city by the same name. Rome was the Babylon of the first century. Cultures in which the false trinity of the dragon, beast, and false prophet thrive are Babylon today. We find her not only by the Euphrates but also by the Potomac. She is doomed. The church is commissioned to announce her doom. This is part of her victory.

The third measure of victory involves the commission to announce the impending doom of the world opposed to Christ. "Then another angel, a third one, followed them, saying with a loud voice, 'If anyone worships the beast and his image, and receives a mark on his forehead or on his hand . . . '" (verse 9). The person who follows the beast's thinking and does his bidding is doomed. He will be an eternal memorial to the foolishness of apostasy. The saint's victory involves issuing the warning of verse 10: "He also will drink of the wine of

117

the wrath of God, which is mixed in full strength in the cup of His anger; and he will be tormented with fire and brimstone in the presence of the holy angels and in the presence of the Lamb."

Part Two

We are in the midst of the announcement of the third angel in Revelation 14. Verses 11-12 complete this vision:

> And the smoke of their torment goes up forever and ever; they have no rest day and night, those who worship the beast and his image, and whoever receives the mark of his name. Here is the perseverance of the saints who keep the commandments of God and their faith in Jesus.

God establishes an eternal memorial as the smoke of judgment ascends perpetually for all the universe to behold. Compare Isaiah 66:24 where the saints of heaven observe the death of hell.

> Then they will go forth and look
> On the corpses of the men
> Who have transgressed against Me.
> For their worm will not die
> And their fire will not be quenched;
> And they will be an abhorrence to all mankind.

Perseverance is part of the victory of God's people. Under all forms of stress and pressure they maintain their faith in Christ and follow the commandments of God. Perseverance involves both. "Faith without works is dead" (James 2:26). This perseverance brings blessing.

"And I heard a voice from heaven, saying, 'Write, "Blessed are the dead who die in the Lord from now on!"' 'Yes,' says the Spirit, 'so that they may rest from their labors, for their deeds follow with t h e m ' " (v e r s e 1 3). This second of seven beatitudes divides the sevenfold announcement of victory. Four announcements have been made. Three remain.

Those who persevere are blessed. It is a blessing to die in the Lord. The phrase "from now on" causes some consternation. Perhaps we should connect these words with the first part of the sentence. "Blessed are the dead from now on." There will be no change in their state of blessedness. They find rest from the labors and rigors of this life. They took the words of Jesus in Matthew 6:20 quite seriously: "Store up for yourselves treasures in heaven, where neither moth nor rust destroys, and where thieves do not break in or steal." The fruit of their lives in Christ follows them. The blessing of heaven awaits all those who keep the faith and exhibit that faith by keeping the commandments.

The scene changes with a vision of the Son of Man reaping His harvest at the end of the age. Verse 14: "Then I looked, and behold, a white cloud, and sitting on the cloud was one like a son of man, having a golden crown on His head and a sharp sickle in His hand." This vision reminds us of Daniel 7:13, "I kept looking in the night visions, and behold, with the clouds of heaven One like a Son of Man was coming, and He came up to the Ancient of Days and was presented before Him." Christ is on His throne. In Revelation, He wears a crown. He reigns. He has a sharp curved knife fit for cutting shocks of grain or clusters of grapes. He awaits the time of the final harvest.

An angel brings the awaited command. This is the fifth announcement of victory. Verse 15: "And another angel came out of the temple, crying out with a loud voice to Him who sat on the cloud, 'Put in your sickle and reap, for the hour to reap has come, because the harvest of the earth is ripe.'"

Jesus confessed, "But of that day and hour no one knows, not even the angels of heaven, nor the Son, but the Father alone" (Matthew 24:36). As the Son of Man, Christ awaits the signal from the Father.

A messenger emerges from the temple with the command of God. Now is the time. The harvest is ripe. The Son of Man takes action. "Then He who sat on the cloud swung His sickle over the earth, and the earth was reaped" (verse 16). The drama is heightened by the simplicity of the narrative. It takes one insertion of the knife and all the earth yields her fruit to the Christ of God.

In this case, it is good fruit. The harvest is ripe from two perspectives. There must be a harvest of God's people sowed with the seed of God's Word. The elect people of God are brought in by the everlasting gospel. There must also be a harvest of judgment when the cup of sin is filled by the reprobate of the earth. The description of this harvest follows. Christ reigns. He is the victor. His people share in His work.

The mere appearance of another angel announces the impending harvest of doom. This is the sixth broadcast of victory. Evil is judged. Righteousness reigns. "And another angel came out of the temple which is in heaven, and he also had a sharp sickle" (verse 17). As Christ and the Father are one and as this angel is an extension of the Father's hand, so he is the hand of Christ weighing in against the evil of the earth.

A final angel caps the sevenfold victory. Verse 18: "Then another angel, the one who has power over fire, came out from the altar; and he called with a loud voice to him who had the sharp sickle, saying, "Put in your sharp sickle and gather the clusters from the vine of the earth, because her grapes are ripe."

This is the angel we met in chapter eight who poured incense on the altar representing the prayers of God's people who seek judgment. Compare Revelation 6:9-11. In answer to these prayers of the saints, this angel took fire from the altar and cast it upon the earth (Revelation 8:5). Now he calls for the fire of judgment in a different form: "Put in your knife." "So the angel swung his sickle to the earth and gathered the clusters from the vine of the earth, and threw them into the great winepress of the wrath of God" (verse 19). Judgment is often pictured by a winepress. This is God's winepress. These words remind us of God's judgment on Tyre and Sidon. "Put in the sickle, for the harvest is ripe. Come, tread, for the winepress is full; the vats overflow, for their wickedness is great" (Joel 3:13). "And the winepress was trodden outside the city, and blood came out from the winepress, up to the horses' bridles, for a distance of two hundred miles" (verse 20).

Christ died outside the city. There He took the judgment due to others for their sin. There was no escape for Him. There is also no escape for those who are outside of Christ. The Holy City, New Jerusalem, is the ultimate city of refuge for sinners. Those outside perish. Imagine horses struggling in bridle-deep blood. Imagine a sea covering the whole land. There is no escape. This is the picture. This is also the ultimate and perfect victory of Christ in which His people share. Section four of Revelation begins with the birth of Christ. It continues with warfare between God's people and the followers of the false trinity. It ends with the victory of the Son of Man.

God's Perfect Judgments

Revelation 15:1-8

As we continue our look at Revelation in its seven-fold view of the inter-advent period, we once again review the time between the first coming and the second coming of Christ. Different emphases are given to us as we progress through the parallel sections. There is greater emphasis upon the end of this period as we approach the end of the book even as there is great emphasis on the first century at the beginning of the book. Note especially the letters to the seven churches.

Chapters 15 and 16 compose the fifth section of this great book of the Revelation of Jesus Christ. In it we witness the seven last plagues in the seven bowls of wrath. Chapter 15 introduces the seven bowls of wrath. Chapter 16 displays them in all their fury. "And I saw another sign in heaven, great and marvelous, seven angels who had seven plagues, which are the last, because in them the wrath of God is finished" (Revelation 15:1). This verse is similar to Revelation 12:1, "And a great sign appeared in heaven." These two verses are the only ones in Revelation where the Spirit describes the *sign* as *great*. Revelation 12:1 obviously begins a new section of the book. The similarity of Revelation 15:1 argues that it too begins a section of the book.

We again see the significance of the number seven. There are seven angels and seven plagues. These are the *last*. That is, in them, the wrath of God is perfected. No plague can be added to them.

These plagues also descend from heaven throughout the present age. Romans 1:18 tells us this: "For the wrath of God is revealed from heaven against all ungodliness and unrighteousness of men who suppress the truth in unrighteousness." The wrath of God comes to perfection in different lives, in various ways, and at distinct times. This is the import of the number seven.

Verse 2 continues: "And I saw something like a sea of glass mixed with fire, and those who had been victorious over the beast and his image and the number of his name, standing on the sea of glass, holding harps of God." This is the sea of glass upon which we saw the throne of God (Revelation 4:6). The sea of nations is calm under God's acknowledged rule. The sea is also covered with the flames of affliction, trial, and suffering. Compare 1 Peter 4:12. "Beloved, do not be surprised at the fiery ordeal among you, which comes upon you for your testing, as though some strange thing were happening to you."

There are individuals standing on the sea of glass in the midst of the flames of affliction. They stood against the beast, his image, and the number of his name. They are victors. The beast is anti-Christian power manifest in government and political power. The image of the beast is a complex of institutions built on ungodly principles. This image provides a mouth for the false prophet in schools, laboratories, museums, publishing companies, theaters, television networks, etc. "They overcame him [the dragon and his henchmen] because of the blood of the Lamb and because of the word of their testimony, and they did not love their life even when faced with death" (Revelation 12:11).

One of the signs of their victory is that they are "holding harps of God." Because this is a picture, these are not literal harps. These harps symbolize the Spirit empowered praise of God's people. Verses 3-4:

> And they sang the song of Moses, the bond-servant of God, and the song of the Lamb, saying, "Great and marvelous are Your works, O Lord God, the Almighty; righteous and true are Your ways, King of the nations! Who will not fear, O Lord, and glorify Your name for You alone are holy; for all the nations will come and worship before You, for Your righteous acts have been revealed."

Note the two-fold nature of the song sung by these saints. It is one song. It is a song of redemption. It is the same redemption viewed in prospect in the Old Testament and in fulfillment in the New Testament. There is one salvation and one salvation song. The song of Moses and the song of Jesus do not differ.

God is the Righteous One. He is King. His ways are true. His story as revealed by Christ is most righteous and holy. All peoples will one day acknowledge this either willingly in heaven or by constraint in hell (Philippians 2:9-11).

We now realize we have an extraordinary view of the sacred precincts of heaven open before us. Verses 5-6: "After these things I looked, and the temple of the tabernacle of testimony in heaven was opened, and the seven angels who had the seven plagues came out of the temple, clothed in linen, clean and bright, and girded around their chests with golden sashes."

The seven angels were within the temple of God before His throne. Now we see a recessional. The angels come out from the central dwelling place of God. The testimony of God's grace and the testimony of God's judgments come from this temple. The angels bear the image of Christ (Revelation 1:13). They represent Him in His judgments.

Verse 7: "Then one of the four living creatures gave to the seven angels seven golden bowls full of the wrath of God, who lives forever and ever." One of the living creatures closest to the throne distributes golden bowls of wrath. This wrath comes from God. Oddly, from a human perspective, the golden bowls show wrath is a valuable commodity. Can it be so? It is certainly of high value from God's perspective.

We see this as verse 8 continues the description and shows us once again that grace and judgment always accompany each other. "And the temple was filled with smoke from the glory of God and from His power; and no one was able to enter the temple until the seven plagues of the seven angels were finished." The heavenly temple, into which we have been privileged to peer is now shrouded with smoke. We cannot see into it. The text says no one is able to enter it either. The plagues of God, His wrath poured out, must be completed. There is a perfect end for which this wrath is designed.

In Jesus Christ we see sin punished by wrath poured out *upon Him*. This is grace. Those who heed the warning trumpets of God turn to Christ. Wrath due to *them* falls *upon Him*. The temple is opened for us only when wrath against our sin is finished. For others, wrath for sin in hell is never finished.

Pour Out the Seven Bowls

Revelation 16:1-12

We now turn directly to the seven bowls of wrath. These bowls of wrath are contemporaneous to the seven trumpets. How so? Those who refuse to heed the perfect warnings of God to repent (Revelation 9:20-21) experience the wrath of God perfectly brought to bear upon them as individuals and nations.

The bowls of wrath are more severe judgments descending upon the earth than we have seen in earlier cases. There are two reasons for this. Inevitably, the judgments of God become more severe and more pervasive as hearts harden and men and women refuse to repent. Witness the plagues against Egypt and Pharaoh's hardness.

Revelation 16:1: "Then I heard a loud voice from the temple, saying to the seven angels, 'Go and pour out on the earth the seven bowls of the wrath of God.'" After the angels are prepared, God commands the pouring out of wrath. Is God the God of love? Yes, He is. We must remember the good God has a good reason for wrath. God is the God of justice. Perfect justice is being and will be meted out by Him. Wrath comes as a part of God's plans and purposes.

Verse 2: "So the first angel went and poured out his bowl on the earth; and it became a loathsome and malignant sore on the people who had the mark of the beast and who worshipped his image."

Notice the similarity between the trumpets and the bowls of wrath. The first trumpet sounds a warning against the earth (Revelation 8:7). The first angel pours the first bowl of wrath on the earth. There is also dissimilarity. In this case, there is no restraint upon God's judgments. In the former case a third of the fruit of the earth was destroyed (8:7). Under the fourth seal, one fourth of the earth felt the brunt of God's discipline (6:8). When men and women do not have ears to hear God working in providence to call them back to Himself, He speaks progressively louder.

The earth symbolizes the world opposed to God. It is the kingdom of the devil. Men and women within it have the mark of the beast; they bear the fruit of the unholy spirit, the deeds of the flesh. These people have a deadly cancer of the soul which will never be healed.

"The second angel poured out his bowl into the sea, and it became blood like that of a dead man; and every living thing in the sea died" (verse 3). Again, compare the second trumpet's warning against the sea (8:8-9). In Revelation, the sea is an image of the tumult of the nations without Christ. When the warning trumpet goes unheeded, peoples, tribes, tongues and nations are doomed. One third of the fruits of the sea are destroyed in the warning (8:8-9). Now, "*every* living thing in the sea died."

Verse 4: "Then the third angel poured out his bowl into the rivers and the springs of waters; and they became blood." Compare again the third trumpet where a third of the rivers and of the springs of waters became bitter (8:10-11). The rivers and wells of Egypt were turned to blood (Exodus 7:19-20). Water is absolutely essential to life. The water of the Spirit is absolutely essential to eternal life. Without it there is eternal death. Verses 5-6: "And I heard the angel of the waters saying, 'Righteous are You, who are and who were, O Holy One, because You judged these things; for they poured out the blood of saints and prophets, and You have given them blood to drink. They deserve it.'"

We have previously seen the angel having power over fire (8:5, 14:8). There were also the angels holding back the four winds (7:1). Now we see the angel of the waters. This angel sings a song of God's justice. The reprobate receive God's justice because they deserve it. This is always the case in God's economy. Mercy on the other hand is undeserved. Mercy on the basis of merit is not mercy (Romans 11:6). There are, much to our wondering eyes, vessels of wrath and vessels of mercy (Romans 9:22-23). Mercy is therefore properly understood against this backdrop of deserved wrath.

Verse 7: "And I heard the altar saying, 'Yes, O Lord God, the Almighty, true and righteous are Your judgments.'" The saints under the altar revealed by the fifth seal (6:9-11) rejoice at the judgments of God. We will see this joy over judgment in graphic relief after the description of Babylon's fall (19:1-6). The righteous avenging of evil is a vital part of God's divine plan. First century saints needed to know this as well as twenty-first century Christians.

The fourth angel now empties his golden bowl of wrath. "The fourth angel poured out his bowl upon the sun, and it was given to it to scorch men with fire. Men were scorched with fierce heat; and they blasphemed the name of God who has the power over these plagues, and they did not repent so as to give Him glory" (verses 8-9).

Under the fourth trumpet, a third of the sun, moon and stars were darkened. Light from heaven was withdrawn. Common grace was diminished. As this occurs, violence increases. We see the complement under the fourth bowl of wrath. God brings the heat of the Sun of Righteousness (Malachi 4:2) to bear upon unrepentant sinners. The result is burning consciences. There is vile enmity because of revealed sin. Further hardness follows the blaspheme. So it is among unregenerate haters of God. They love darkness rather than light. Their judgment involves light piercing their evil consciences and causing sharp pain.

"Then the fifth angel poured out his bowl on the throne of the beast, and his kingdom became darkened; and they gnawed their tongues because of pain, and they blasphemed the God of heaven because of their pains and their sores; and they did not repent of their deeds" (verses 10-11).

The fifth trumpet involved locusts from the abyss tormenting those of the earth. This was a warning. The torments were restricted and the warnings unperfected. There is no escape. There is no repentance. Those not loving light are given eternal darkness. Because they willingly wallowed in the deeds of the flesh in this life, they are given what they desire in the life to come, more of the same. Their consciences then burn forever. Their loathing of God and His people increase exponentially and eternally. This is perfect frightful judgment.

Armageddon

Revelation 16:13-16

The similarity between the first five bowls of wrath and the first five trumpets continues. The sixth bowl of wrath and the sixth trumpet refer to the Euphrates.

> Then the sixth angel sounded, and I heard a voice from the four horns of the golden altar which is before God, one saying to the sixth angel who had the trumpet, 'Release the four angels who are bound at the great river Euphrates.' And the four angels, who had been prepared for the hour and day and month and year, were released, so that they would kill a third of mankind (Revelation 9:13-15).

The Euphrates, the eastern extremity and boarder of the ancient kingdom of Israel, represents the boundary between the church and the world. When that border is moved or breached, the world floods the church.

The sixth angel of wrath reveals a similar picture. Verse 12: "The sixth angel poured out his bowl on the great river, the Euphrates; and its water was dried up, so that the way would be prepared for the kings from the east." Paganism is thus poised to flood the kingdom. When pagan, ungodly, and anti-Christian ways push into the kingdom, war is inevitable. In the Old Testament, the combat was often physical conflict. In the New Testament the accent is on spiritual battle. The opening of borders, the lowering of defenses, the removal of the clear distinction between the world and the church inevitably leads to Armageddon.

> And I saw coming out of the mouth of the dragon and out of the mouth of the beast and out of the mouth of the false prophet, three unclean spirits like frogs; for they are spirits of demons, performing signs, which go out to the kings of the whole world, to gather them together for the war of the great day of God, the Almighty (Revelation 16: 13-14).

We again meet the false trinity introduced in chapters 12 and 13. We reviewed the interpretation of the beast and false prophet in the discussion of chapter 15. The signs are seemingly miraculous outworkings of worldly wisdom in education, science and entertainment. The pseudo-trinity spews deception. The frogs are deceiving spirits. First Kings 22 gives an example of how evil spiritual forces may draw people into war:

> The Lord said, "Who will entice Ahab to go up and fall at Ramoth-gilead?" And one said this while another said that. Then a spirit came forward and stood before the Lord and said, "I will entice him." The Lord said to him, "How?" And he said, "I will go out and be a deceiving spirit in the mouth of all his prophets." Then He said, "You are to entice him and also prevail. Go and do so" (Verses 20-22).

Revelation 16:15 is the third of the seven beatitudes in Revelation.[56] It is a call to be on guard, to seek the righteousness of God, to remain unspotted from the world *while under the fire of persecution.* The forces of the world are arrayed against God and His anointed (Psalm 2:2). Verse 15 is parenthetical giving hope to those under these fires of persecution. ("Behold, I am coming like a thief. Blessed is the one who stays awake and keeps his clothes, so that he will not walk about naked and men will not see his shame.")

Where do the princes and kings of the earth assemble with their armies? Verse 16 tells us. "And they gathered them together to the place which in Hebrew is called Har-Magedon." The name means literally Mount of Megiddo. Megiddo is actually located in a broad valley, the Valley of Jezreel, forming a broad plain in northern Israel. Mount Carmel is at the mouth of the valley on the Mediterranean. It was a place of significant and decisive battles in the Old Testament. These Old Testament conflicts and Armageddons typify the cataclysmic spiritual battles in which we may all be involved. Judges 4 relates one of these battles.

> Then the sons of Israel again did evil in the sight of the Lord, after Ehud died. And the Lord sold them into the hand of Jabin king of Canaan . . . Deborah, a prophetess, the wife of Lappidoth, was judging Israel at that time . . . Now she sent and summoned Barak the son of Abinoam . . . So Barak went down from Mount Tabor with ten thousand men following him. The Lord routed Sisera and all his chariots and all his army with the edge of the sword before Barak (Verses 1-15).

Where was this victory won? The song of Judges 5:19 tells us. "The kings came and fought; then fought the kings of Canaan at Taanach near the waters of Megiddo." This victory at Megiddo was a decisive battle, an Armageddon.

A great renewal of Mosaic worship occurred under King Josiah. Before him there was no king like him who turned to the Lord with all his heart and with all his soul and with all his might, according to all the law of Moses; nor did any like him arise after him (2 Kings 23:25).

Yet the sins of Israel were piled to heaven. "However, the Lord did not turn from the fierceness of His great wrath with which His anger burned against Judah" (2 Kings 23:26). And so we read,

> In his days Pharaoh Neco king of Egypt went up to the king of Assyria to the river Euphrates. And King Josiah went to meet him, and when Pharaoh Neco saw him he killed him at Megiddo. His servants drove his body in a chariot from Megiddo, and brought him to Jerusalem and buried him in his own tomb (2 Kings 23:29-30).

The judgment of God consumed King Josiah. The captivity of God's people ensued. This was a climactic battle at Megiddo turning the course of history for God's people. It was an Armageddon.

---

[56] See Pages 167 ff. for an exposition of these seven beatitudes.

Armageddons are decisive climactic battles changing the course of personal, national, or cultural history. These Armageddons are decisive climactic *spiritual* battles fought by saints and churches in our day.

Armageddon is symbolic of decisive climactic battles in which God destroys hypocrisy and Christ rides to victory in our lives. To reveal His grace, mercy, power, holiness, righteousness, and justice, God's purposes involve the revelation of evil, the sovereign salvation of sinners, and the judgment of evil doers. Conflict and struggle may be and must be expected. Armageddons must come. In them saints are perfected. In them the reprobate are punished. In the midst of them we must stay our course remembering the beatitude, "Blessed is the one who stays awake and keeps his clothes."

It Is Done

Revelation 16:17-21

The seventh bowl of wrath brings us once again to the final judgment. We just had a brief interlude, Armageddon. Between the sixth and seventh seals there was also an interlude, the numbering of the 144,000, the church militant, and a vision of the church triumphant (chapter 7). Similarly, between the sixth and seventh trumpets we saw the victory of the gospel through the church militant.

The end comes under the sixth seal with these words, "And God shall wipe every tear from their eyes" (7:17). Compare Revelation 21:4. The seventh seal reveals the seven trumpets. Under the seventh trumpet, "The kingdom of the world has become the kingdom of our Lord and of His Christ; and He will reign forever and ever" (11:15). "And the temple of God which is in heaven was opened" (11:19). Again we are at the end of time. Revelation 16:17: "Then the seventh angel poured out his bowl upon the air, and a loud voice came out of the temple from the throne, saying, 'It is done.'" The judgments of the Lord are perfect. They cover earth, sea, and air. There is no escape. This symbolism ought not to escape us. With the pouring out of the seventh golden bowl, God's wrath is complete. "It is done."

That wrath is perfected implies eternal torment and agony continues. Wrath is complete and perfected even as salvation was fully affected by Christ. The effects linger for eternity. Our Lord Jesus uttered similar words on the cross. "Therefore when Jesus had received the sour wine, He said, 'It is finished!' and He bowed His head and gave up His spirit" (John 19:30). The work of redemption was complete. Christ lived the perfect life required by the Law on behalf of the elect. "So you shall keep My statutes and My judgments, by which a man may live if he does them; I am the Lord" (Leviticus 18:5). Christ also died to pay for the sins of His people (Deuteronomy 21:23, Galatians 3:13). Christ's works of obedience were completed on the cross. "It is finished." Bliss ensues for the elect because Christ concluded His work. Eternal agony results because of God's judgments. Psalm 19:9 says of this wrath, "The judgments of the Lord are true; they are righteous altogether." God makes no mistakes. He makes no errors in judgment. Pun intended. So the seventh angel exclaims, "It is done."

The following verses describe this final cataclysmic judgment. Verse 18: "And there were flashes of lightning and sounds and peals of thunder; and there was a great earthquake, such as there had not been since man came to be upon the earth, so great an earthquake was it, and so mighty."

We recall the flashes of lightning and peals of thunder in the throne room scene of chapter 4. "Out from the throne come flashes of lightning and sounds and peals of thunder" (Revelation 4:5). This was a foretaste of God's judgments. The four living creatures around the throne of God also speak with voices of thunder as they call forth the four horsemen of the apocalypse. The thunder sounds again in response to the prayers of God's people for the vengeance of God. "Then the angel took the censer and filled it with the fire of the altar, and threw it to the earth; and there followed peals of thunder and sounds and flashes of lightning and an earthquake" (Revelation 8:5).

The earthquake is also a dramatic symbol of God's judgment and shaking of the created order. There is an earthquake under the sixth seal (6:12). There is an earthquake, as just seen, in response to the prayers of God's people for judgment. There is an earthquake when the temple in heaven is opened (11:19). Remember, "No one was able to enter the temple until the seven plagues of the seven angels were finished" (15:8). This is all symbolic of Christ's shaking this creation. In Haggai 2:21-22, God promised, "I am going to shake the heavens and the earth. I will overthrow the thrones of kingdoms and destroy the power of the kingdoms of the nations."

Christ fulfilled this prophecy in part at His first coming. He will complete the fulfillment at His second coming. Here is the divine interpretation of Haggai.

> And His voice shook the earth then, but now He has promised, saying, "Yet once more I will shake not only the earth, but also the heaven." This expression, "Yet once more," denotes the removing of those things which can be shaken, as of created things, so that those things which cannot be shaken may remain. Therefore, since we receive a kingdom which cannot be shaken, let us show gratitude, by which we may offer to God an acceptable service with reverence and awe; for our God is a consuming fire (Hebrews 12:26-29).

The earthy gives way to the eternal through Jesus Christ. "The kingdom of the world has become the kingdom of our Lord and of His Christ; and He will reign forever and ever" (11:15).

Verse 19: "The great city was split into three parts, and the cities of the nations fell. Babylon the great was remembered before God, to give her the cup of the wine of His fierce wrath." The great city is Jerusalem "which mystically is called Sodom and Egypt, where also their Lord was crucified" (11:8). It is the apostate visible church. Judgment begins here (1 Peter 4:17). Babylon is the capital of evil encapsulating the work of the dragon, beast, and false prophet. Babylon is doomed (14:8).

Verse 21: "And every island fled away, and the mountains were not found." The way is prepared for the coming of Christ (Isaiah 40:4, Luke 3:5). He brings ultimate judgment and ultimate mercy. Verse 22: "And huge hailstones, about one hundred pounds each, came down from heaven upon men; and men blasphemed God because of the plague of the hail, because its plague was extremely severe." God judged Egypt and Israel with hail (Exodus 9:18-26, Haggai 2:17). Here hail is *symbolic* of judgment. Hundred pound hailstones indicate the massive character of the wrath pour out. It is inescapable. May we heed the voice of God in providence when we see lightning, hear thunder, witness devastating hail. May we remember eternity looms large. May we therefore repent and align ourselves with the Lamb who was slain and yet lives.

130

With the seventh bowl of wrath poured out, judgment is complete. The fifth rehearsal of the inter-advent period is also complete.

The Mystery of Babylon

Revelation 17:1-9

We continue to look at Revelation as a seven-fold view of the inter-advent period, the time between the first coming and the second coming of Christ. As just mentioned, Revelation 16:21 brought us once again to the judgment at the end of the present age. As we draw closer to the end of Revelation, the visions place more emphasis on events at the close of this age. Revelation 14:8 mentions the fall of Babylon. Revelation 16:19 reminds us Babylon is judged already. We step back once again. Revelation 17-19 gives a detailed account of this judgment. Then Revelation 20-22 reveals the final victory of Christ with His bride. Revelation 17:1-2:

> Then one of the seven angels who had the seven bowls came and spoke with me, saying, "Come here, I will show you the judgment of the great harlot who sits on many waters, with whom the kings of the earth committed acts of immorality, and those who dwell on the earth were made drunk with the wine of her immorality."

Revelation 21:9 introduces the bride of Christ with the same words. "Then one of the seven angels who had the seven bowls full of the seven last plagues came and spoke with me, saying, 'Come here, I will show you the bride, the wife of the Lamb.'" Angels with the *last plagues* bid John to view marvelous things. That these particular angels beckon indicates we are discussing the final chapters of history.

Babylon is the capital of evil. She is the center of unrighteousness. She sits on many waters. The waters are the families and nations outside of Christ. "The waters which you saw where the harlot sits, are peoples and multitudes and nations and tongues" (17:15). Those drunk with her immoralities are those who follow the ways of the world in every area of life in opposition to Christ. The kings mentioned are leaders in medicine, science, education, religion, and government. Babylon's counterpart is the New Jerusalem, the bride of Christ, the center of the manifestation of righteousness in creation.

Verse 3: "And he carried me away in the Spirit into a wilderness; and I saw a woman sitting on a scarlet beast, full of blasphemous names, having seven heads and ten horns." The dragon, the serpent of old, proudly carries the woman into battle in the wilderness (Revelation 12:6). She dresses as royalty. Babylon is the queen of evil. The world bows before her opulence and seeks with might and main to partake of her luxury.

Verse 4: "The woman was clothed in purple and scarlet, and adorned with gold and precious stones and pearls, having in her hand a gold cup full of abominations and of the unclean things of her immorality." The cup she carries is full of uncleanness. It is a gold cup. Gold, precious to the ungodly, symbolizes how precious immorality is to the fallen world.

Babylon carries a name written on her forehead. This is her seal, her identifying mark. It corresponds to the mark of the beast. It describes her character. Verse 5: "And on her forehead a name was written, a mystery, 'BABYLON THE GREAT, THE MOTHER OF HARLOTS AND OF THE ABOMINATIONS OF THE EARTH.'" Babylon is not simply the apostate church. Her name includes *all the abominations of the earth.* It might well be that the words *a mystery* are part of the name. In Scripture, a mystery is something unveiled. Here we see lewd, licentious, bawdy Babylon unveiled in judgment.

Remember, we are looking at a vision. We see symbols. They represent reality. The reality is that the world outside of Christ is intoxicated with itself and with sin. As seen in previous visions, the world is in mortal combat with the church. No subterfuge is withheld in the battle against righteousness and godliness. This is the portrayal verse 6 gives: "And I saw the woman drunk with the blood of the saints, and with the blood of the witnesses of Jesus. When I saw her, I wondered greatly." The world stands in awe of the greatness and luxury of Babylon. Why should the church and the saints be amazed at her power and strength?

Verse 7 therefore broaches the question to John. "And the angel said to me, 'Why do you wonder? I will tell you the mystery of the woman and of the beast that carries her, which has the seven heads and the ten horns.'" The mystery of Babylon now comes to light. Men and women should not worship at her throne nor drink of her cup. In today's world one of the manifestations of Babylon is athletics. The recent Olympic Games in Atlanta in the United States were presented as an extension of ancient Greek paganism. The hope was for world peace and unity to emerge. Yet the Bible plainly says with reference to Christ, "For He Himself is our peace" (Ephesians 2:14). We cannot have it both ways.

Although many Christians participated in the Olympic Games, those Games were not *the* answer to the sin-based dilemmas of our world. Why do worldly institutions take on this messianic complex? In the end, they are servants of the devil.

Verse 8: "The beast that you saw was, and is not, and is about to come up out of the abyss and go to destruction. And those who dwell on the earth, whose name has not been written in the book of life from the foundation of the world, will wonder when they see the beast, that he was and is not and will come."

There is a resurrection of sorts portrayed here. I do not think this is an actual resurrection of an actual entity or person. I think this simply pictures the dragon and his rider as a false Christ, a false messiah, to whom the world flees and in whom the world puts its trust.

The dragon and the woman are doomed. The earth, representative of those who oppose Christ, is also doomed. They are reprobate. Their names are not and never were in the book of life. The reprobate marvel at the splendor of Babylon. Americans marvel at and venerate Olympic, college, and professional athletes. Cities and communities dream of championship teams. Attracting good athletes is big business. Is this a covert repudiation of Providence and the God of Providence? Is this worship of the creature rather than the Creator who is blessed forever?

Babylon, The Great City

Revelation 17:9-18

I maintain the best way to interpret the visions before us is to recognize the deeply symbolic nature of Revelation. We see pictures portraying reality not the reality itself. Keeping this in mind, we begin this section of exposition with Revelation 17:9-10.

"Here is the mind which has wisdom. The seven heads are seven mountains on which the woman sits, and they are seven kings; five have fallen, one is, the other has not yet come; and when he comes, he must remain a little while." Within the vision an interpretation is given. This interpretation is also symbolic as it is also part of the vision.

The seven heads of the dragon are seven mountains. Many commentators insist the seven mountains are the seven hills of Rome and that this fixes the identity of Babylon. As previously seen, mountains often represent kingdoms. Here are seven kingdoms. Why seven? This is a number of completeness. The dragon and the woman have complete power within their domain. Only the intervention of the Sovereign God can extricate peoples and families from this evil power. This is the glory of the Gospel. Christ plunders the strong man's house and takes captive a people for himself.

Continuing our interpretation, Babylon is the capital of evil. New Jerusalem is the capital of righteousness. We have the City of Man versus the City of God. Ancient Babylon was on the Euphrates. Surely contemporary Babylon for first century Christians was Rome located on the Tiber. However, realize this: "Babylon is with us in every age . . . Thus Babylon must be seen not only on the Thames, the Seine, the Rhine, the Volga, and the Bosphorus and the Nile but also on the Potomac."[57]

Washington, D.C. is every bit a modern Babylon as Rome once was. This is a bitter pill for Americans to swallow. Sadly, many Christian fundamentalists wrongly equate Americanism and Christianity. Were the USA a Christian nation bowing to Christ by conviction and constitution, the story would be far different. This is not the case. Christ calls us to be light in the world of North America and salt in the earth of North America.

Further description follows in verse 11. "The beast which was and is not, is himself also an eighth and is one of the seven, and he goes to destruction." The dragon and his kingdoms are set for destruction. Those caught up in worldliness are fools. They have eyes for nothing else. Psalm 92:6-7 prophesies this. We must grasp and be warned by this truth:

A senseless man has no knowledge,
Nor does a stupid man understand this:

---

[57] Rousas John Rushdoony, *Thy Kingdom Come* (Nutley, N.J.: Presbyterian and Reformed, 1970), 180.

That when the wicked sprouted up like grass
And all who did iniquity flourished,
It was only that they might be destroyed forevermore.

This is the ordained destiny of unbelief. Other worldly kingdoms will follow. They will round out the divine plan, ten horns are ten kingdoms. These kings and kingdoms are servants of the dragon, the beast upon which the harlot rides. In terms of eternity, their tenure on earth, enthralled with worldly pleasure, is short. This seems to be the import of verse 12. "The ten horns which you saw are ten kings who have not yet received a kingdom, but they receive authority as kings with the beast for one hour."

I demur. I do not identify these kings as historical characters, Roman Caesars. This is risky at best. Rather, I say, the purpose of worldly kingdoms is to glorify the devil and to wage war with the people of God. Verses 13-14: "These have one purpose, and they give their power and authority to the beast. These will wage war against the Lamb, and the Lamb will overcome them, because He is Lord of lords and King of kings, and those who are with Him are the called and chosen and faithful."

The people of God prevail. The gospel goes forth in victory (Revelation 6:1-2, Psalm 45:4-5). Christ leads His army into battle and to triumph (Revelation 19:11-16). There are "the called and chosen and faithful." God "concerned Himself about taking from among the Gentiles a people for Himself" (Acts 15:14). Those who remain serve the harlot. This is what verse 15 tells us. "And he said to me, 'The waters which you saw where the harlot sits, are peoples and multitudes and nations and tongues.'"

Evil feeds on itself. The kingdoms of this world inevitably fight against one another because they all have one goal, the consolidation of power. War is inevitable. Power struggles within businesses and the church are inevitable. Evil is self defeating. Babylon may be the capital of evil but lesser powers will always vie for her position and prestige. Those who wield ungodly power must have complete control over subordinates as well as their complete loyalty. Managers in businesses insist on loyalty. "Can I trust you?" This is the question. It means, "Will you do anything to enhance my position and power?" It is trust based upon intimidation. It results in conflict and defeat. This is the meaning of verse 16. "And the ten horns which you saw, and the beast, these will hate the harlot and will make her desolate and naked, and will eat her flesh and will burn her up with fire."

All of this fulfills God's plans and purposes. Remember, we are seeing the scroll, the book of God's decrees being opened by Christ, the King of the universe (Revelation 5). Our major purpose is to see the greatness and majesty of God and of Christ. Verse 17: "For God has put it in their hearts to execute His purpose by having a common purpose, and by giving their kingdom to the beast, until the words of God will be fulfilled."

We end Revelation 17 with a simple but dramatic statement. "The woman whom you saw is the great city, which reigns over the kings of the earth" (verse 18). Once again we see Babylon is the capital of evil in every age. Jerusalem of old turned to whoredom. She capitulated to Rome and repudiated Christ and the gospel. The great city became Babylon. Compare Revelation 11:8. Hence the need for New Jerusalem to come down from heaven. Revelation 17 gives an overview of the destruction of Babylon. Revelation 18 gives greater detail.

Fallen, Fallen is Babylon

Revelation 18:1-10

Now we zero in on the judgment of Babylon. Revelation 18:1: "After these things I saw another angel coming down from heaven, having great authority, and the earth was illumined with his glory."

This messenger from heaven is glorious. He is part of the highest echelons of heaven. His presence illumines the earth. Again I say, the earth represents that evil spiritual world system dominated by Satan. This is a picture of real spiritual illumination coming to the world by way of common grace. The purpose of this illumination is that men and women will really see the demise of Babylon. Such illumination can and does come today through the preaching of the law and gospel. In fact, the Bible charges us to provide such light (Ephesians 5:7-14).

Verse 2 brings the awesome announcement of the glorious angel. "And he cried out with a mighty voice, saying, 'Fallen, fallen is Babylon the great! She has become a dwelling place of demons and a prison of every unclean spirit, and a prison of every unclean and hateful bird.'"

What is the problem of Babylon? Look through her gates and you peer into the depths and darkness of hell erupting into the affairs of humankind. A description of the problem continues in verse 3.

"For all the nations have drunk of the wine of the passion of her immorality, and the kings of the earth have committed acts of immorality with her, and the merchants of the earth have become rich by the wealth of her sensuality."

Men and women, families, nations and governments spurn the Bible, the God of the Bible, and the gospel of the Bible. They grasp after the hope of greater wealth and the gospel of better education. They trust secularism and atheistic humanism, the doctrines of demons (1 Timothy 4:1). Verses 4-5: "I heard another voice from heaven, saying, 'Come out of her, my people, so that you will not participate in her sins and receive of her plagues.' For her sins have piled up as high as heaven, and God has remembered her iniquities."

There is a call familiar to all Christians. Who issues the call? Perhaps an angel speaking on behalf of God. Paul quotes Jeremiah 51:45 to this effect in 2 Corinthians 6:17: "Therefore, 'Come out from their midst and be separate, says the Lord. And do not touch what is unclean; and I will welcome you.'"

The context in Jeremiah is separation from Babylon and a return to Jerusalem and the true worship of God. The context in 2 Corinthians is separation from unbelief, immorality, and darkness and a return to God in proper worship. This seems to substantiate the direction of our interpretation. Believers must separate themselves from Babylon in all her tempting manifestations because God sees her sins and His judgment looms large. They must be fully aligned with the New Jerusalem in the worship of the majestic Christ.

Verse 6 continues the direction from heaven for judgment. The direction is probably given to the angels charged with carrying it out under the seven trumpets and seven bowls of wrath. "Pay her back even as she has paid, and give back to her double according to her deeds; in the cup which she has mixed, mix twice as much for her."

The sins of Babylon come to culmination as was the case with the Amorites of old. "Then in the fourth generation they will return here, for the iniquity of the Amorite is not yet complete" (Genesis 15:16). As Babylon doubles her efforts to sin, God doubles her judgment. In strict accordance to her sin God judges. Jesus said it, "I tell you that every careless word that people speak, they shall give an accounting for it in the day of judgment" (Matthew 12:36). Compare also Jeremiah 16:18 and 17:18 and their contexts. Double or twofold judgment is complete judgment.

Verses 7-8 confirm this: "To the degree that she glorified herself and lived sensuously, to the same degree give her torment and mourning; for she says in her heart, 'I sit as a queen and I am not a widow, and will never see mourning.'" The punishment fits the crime. The great crime is arrogance. The pride of unbelief exalts itself to the level of God. It is a worship of self, the creature, rather than the Creator.

This arrogance and the concomitant actions demand God's answer. Therefore verse 8 continues the pronouncement of the voice from heaven begun in verse 4. "For this reason in one day her plagues will come, pestilence and mourning and famine, and she will be burned up with fire; for the Lord God who judges her is strong." Judgment will be swift. God is the real "strong man."

There is dramatic response to this sudden judgment of the world system represented by Babylon. Verses 9-10:

> And the kings of the earth, who committed acts of immorality and lived sensuously with her, will weep and lament over her when they see the smoke of her burning, standing at a distance because of the fear of her torment, saying, "Woe, woe, the great city, Babylon, the strong city! For in one hour your judgment has come."

The first category of people, leaders in the world system, reacts with astonishment. These are leaders in anti-Christian science, education, arts, entertainment, government, and religion. Because of common grace, they truly fear the torment they see. Cries of agony and despair come from their lips, "Woe, woe."

The word *burning* in the phrase *the smoke of her burning* is significant. The apostle uses it 1 Peter 4:12. "Beloved, do not be surprised at the *fiery ordeal* among you, which comes upon you for your testing, as though some strange thing were happening to you" (italics added).

Fiery ordeals involve physical torment, emotional distress, or spiritual anguish. They test the reality and sincerity of faith. Compare Matthew 13:20-21. Christians are not exempt from persecution and affliction. Cancer and the need for hip replacements are common among believers. These same fiery ordeals become judgments against unbelief. For believers there is deliverance from them all. For the reprobate these same afflictions are magnified infinitely in perdition. Seeing this horrifies reprobate observers. This fear is part of their torment.

The long expected, sought, and prayed for judgment comes. The saints cried to God for it (Revelation 6:10); they prayed for it (Revelation 8:3-5). They are also to rejoice in it (Revelation 18:20).

Rejoice Over Her, O Heaven

Revelation 18:11-24

The first category of those watching in horror the judgment of their beloved city included kings, the leaders. Now we have the second category, merchants. The former lead the forces of anti-Christ. The latter willingly carry the anti-Christian message throughout the world. Revelation 18:11: "And the merchants of the earth weep and mourn over her, because no one buys their cargoes any more."

Verses 12-14 indicate the merchants bought and sold. There are seven categories listed. The fullness of the world's treasures was in the hands of these merchants. There are . . .

cargoes of gold and silver and precious stones and pearls and fine linen and purple and silk and scarlet, and every kind of citron wood and every article of ivory and every article made from very costly wood and bronze and iron and marble, and cinnamon and spice and incense and perfume and frankincense and wine and olive oil and fine flour and wheat and cattle and sheep, and cargoes of horses and chariots and slaves and human lives.

Here is the breakdown. One: cargoes of gold and silver and precious stones and pearls; two: fine linen and purple and silk and scarlet; three: every kind of citron wood and every article of ivory and every article made from very costly wood and bronze and iron and marble; four: cinnamon and spice and incense and perfume and frankincense; five: wine and olive oil and fine flour and wheat and cattle and sheep; six: cargoes of horses and chariots; seven: slaves and human lives

What of luxury now? Verse 18 laments its loss: "The fruit you long for has gone from you, and all things that were luxurious and splendid have passed away from you and men will no longer find them."

The purveyors of all worldly goods stand aghast. They tremble at the judgment of Babylon. They have enough light to see the doom of all they thought was good and lasting. They fear because they know they have a part and share in the profits of Babylon. They lament Babylon's fall because it is also their demise.

Verses 15-17:

The merchants of these things, who became rich from her, will stand at a distance because of the fear of her torment, weeping and mourning, "Woe, woe, the great city, she who was clothed in fine linen and purple and scarlet, and adorned with gold and precious stones and pearls; for in one hour such great wealth has been laid waste!"

Those who teach, preach, write, support, and find their livelihood in the things of the world sing a song of woe. This includes all those engaged in the commerce of evil in any way whatsoever.

Revelation 18:17-18 introduce a third group lamenting the fall of Babylon. "And every shipmaster and every passenger and sailor, and as many as make their living by the sea, stood at a distance, and were crying out as they saw the smoke of her burning, saying, 'What city is like the great city?'"

We move down the economic scale from kings to merchants to shipmasters and sailors. The common person is now in view. The common worker may be victimized by his or her leaders and managers. Yet these people too have their part in the propagation of evil. They consent to it and assist in its spread.

When judgment comes, they can ask only one question. "What city is like the great city?" They are amazed at the splendor of Babylon and conceive no other city can be greater. The glory of New Jerusalem escapes their vision. They have no eye for the eternal. Verse 19 shows their dismay.

"And they threw dust on their heads and were crying out, weeping and mourning, saying, 'Woe, woe, the great city, in which all who had ships at sea became rich by her wealth, for in one hour she has been laid waste!'"

The rug of life is ripped out from under these mourners. All they know and lived for is gone. Their world is destroyed. This completes the threefold lament over the fall of Babylon. It is a doleful sound, the most mournful which could be heard.

In verse 20, the voice from heaven introduced in verse 4 exhorts heaven to rejoice over the fall of Babylon. "Rejoice over her, O heaven, and you saints and apostles and prophets, because God has pronounced judgment for you against her."

Can there be joy in heaven over the judgment of evil? There can be no sadness in that blessed place. As we, on an earthly plane, rejoice over the defeat of enemies in war, so there is joy in heaven over the defeat and judgment of Babylon. We witness the justice of God and rejoice. The smoke of Babylon's burning is an eternal testimony to God's justice always visible from New Jerusalem. Compare again Isaiah 66:24.

The scene now shifts to a vision of a strong angel. Verse 21.

"Then a strong angel took up a stone like a great millstone and threw it into the sea, saying, 'So will Babylon, the great city, be thrown down with violence, and will not be found any longer.'"

Earlier, we saw a strong angel cry out to the residents of heaven, earth and hell (Revelation 5:2). He sought someone to open the book with seven seals. We also saw a strong angel with a little book, the gospel, take command of land and sea (Revelation 10:1). The millstone cast into the sea is a sign of final doom (Matthew 9:42, Luke 17:2). The strong angel announces the devastating results of judgment.

Verses 22-24:

And the sound of harpists and musicians and flute-players and trumpeters will not be heard in you any longer; and no craftsman of any craft will be found in

142

you any longer; and the sound of a mill will not be heard in you any longer; and the light of a lamp will not shine in you any longer; and the voice of the bridegroom and bride will not be heard in you any longer; for your merchants were the great men of the earth, because all the nations were deceived by your sorcery. And in her was found the blood of prophets and of saints and of all who have been slain on the earth.

All joy and all reasons for joy are gone. Babylon's doom is sealed. Hallelujah!

The Marriage of the Lamb

Revelation 19:1-8

In Chapter 17, in this sixth section of Revelation, we saw those trapped in unbelief wondering at the fabulous wealth, luxuriant estate, and unbridled decadence of Babylon. In Revelation 18 we saw these same people standing in awe as they witness the destruction of their lives and livelihoods.

The scene now shifts. We see the response of the saints in heaven and on earth to the judgment of the great harlot.

> After these things I heard something like a loud voice of a great multitude in heaven, saying, "Hallelujah! Salvation and glory and power belong to our God; because His judgments are true and righteous; for He has judged the great harlot who was corrupting the earth with her immorality, and He has avenged the blood of His bond-servants on her" (Revelation 19:1-2).

Heaven refers to God's people as earth refers to God's enemies. The voice of a multitude in heaven sings a song celebrating God's judgment.

You recall in the early visions of Revelation God's people call to Him to avenge their blood. They cry from under the altar, "How long, O Lord, holy and true, will You refrain from judging and avenging our blood on those who dwell on the earth?" (Revelation 6:10). The saints now witness the vengeance of God. Their response? Hallelujah! Praise Jehovah. "The judgments of the Lord are true; they are righteous altogether" (Psalm 19:9). The judgment of Babylon bears out the truth and righteousness of God's holy purposes.

Two questions. First, should the saints rejoice over the judgment of men and women who serve evil? Second, will saints in heaven be able to see this judgment? Verse 3 intensifies the questions. "And a second time they said, 'Hallelujah! Her smoke rises up forever and ever.'" The saints of God see the smoke of this judgment "forever and ever."

Regarding question one, have you ever been to a football game or a basketball game of some league or conference significance? On the court or on the field, the opposition is the enemy. Did you rejoice over the defeat of the opposition? Let's carry the analogy to a higher level. At the end of WWII, there was dancing in the streets on V. J. Day. Men and women rightly rejoiced at the defeat and humiliation of Japan. Should we not rejoice when God exacts perfect justice? Yes! We long to see justice. We will rejoice when God's vengeance strikes.

Regarding question two, Jesus likens the smoking pit of Gehenna just outside the wall of Jerusalem to hell. People of the city could look into this Valley of Hinnom and see the smoke rising. This was a picture of final judgment. Revelation 19:3 refers to another such picture. It quotes Isaiah 34:10 and the judgment of Edom.

"Its streams will be turned into pitch, and its loose earth into brimstone, and its land will become burning pitch. It will not be quenched night or day;

144

its smoke will go up forever. From generation to generation it will be desolate" (Isaiah 34:9-10).

Similarly, Isaiah 66:24 pictures men and women able to peer into hell and see the awful judgments of God.

Then they will go forth and look
On the corpses of the men
Who have transgressed against Me.
For their worm will not die
And their fire will not be quenched;
And they will be an abhorrence to all mankind.

Compare Mark 9:47-48 to confirm Isaiah speaks of eternal torment in hell. "If your eye causes you to stumble, throw it out; it is better for you to enter the kingdom of God with one eye, than, having two eyes, to be cast into hell, WHERE THEIR WORM DOES NOT DIE, AND THEIR FIRE IS NOT QUENCHED."

Regarding both questions one and two, the ability of heaven to peer into hell intensifies the praise offered to God for salvation. Not only do men and women see the terrible judgments of God, they realize this is their doom except for Christ. He lived a perfect life on their behalf. He fulfilled the demands of the law—perfect righteousness—for them. He also died in their place to pay the penalty due to them for their sins. They live while others perish. Adoration therefore abounds.

The praise continues in verse 4. "And the twenty-four elders and the four living creatures fell down and worshipped God who sits on the throne saying, 'Amen. Hallelujah!'"

I maintain the twenty-four elders are a high echelon of angels. Compare Revelation 5:9-10 where they sing a song about Christ's redeeming, not of themselves, but God's people. In this text they offer their "Amen" to the rejoicing.

Verse 5 brings a command from the throne at the center of heaven. God calls every saint to give Him praise.

"And a voice came from the throne, saying, 'Give praise to our God, all you His bond-servants, you who fear Him, the small and the great.'"

When we gather for worship, we too are around the throne with the four living creatures, the twenty-four elders, myriads of angels, tens of thousands of glorified saints, and all believers in the world. This is one of the great significances of our worship each Lord's Day. Our citizenship is in heaven. We are part of the choir gathered around the throne. Praise multiplies at the command emanating from the throne.

"Then I heard something like the voice of a great multitude and like the sound of many waters and like the sound of mighty peals of thunder, saying, 'Hallelujah! For the Lord our God, the Almighty, reigns'" (verse 6).

This is the Hallelujah Chorus. The Lord God omnipotent reigns. The sound like Niagara indicates the power of this song. The thunder reveals the judgmental side of God. The songs of the church ought to contain the strains of mercy *and* the sounds of judgments.

Concurrent with the judgment of Babylon is the joy of the church's wedding with Christ. Verse 7: "Let us rejoice and be glad and give the glory to Him, for the marriage of the Lamb has come and His bride has made herself ready." The bride of Christ, arrayed in His righteousness, realizes her privileged estate. Verse 8: "It was given to her to clothe herself in fine linen, bright and clean; for the fine linen is the righteous acts of the saints." These are the righteous acts of the saints *as seen by of God*. He does not see "a filthy garment" (Isaiah 64:6). God sees the righteous acts of His Son imputed to us, given to us as a free gift.

The Great Supper of God

Revelation 19:9-18

The songs of heaven celebrate the consummation, the wedding to which God draws all the new creation. The angel announcing the doom of Babylon (17:1) speaks of this blessing. Verse 9.

"Then he said to me, 'Write, "Blessed are those who are invited to the marriage supper of the Lamb."' And he said to me, 'These are true words of God.'"

Those invited to the marriage supper are the truly blessed. Having a part in this feast is the ultimate. All else pales in insignificance. As we have seen and shall see, the alternative is eternal death in hell. Individuals either enter the temple of God by way of the cross or they participate in the terror of Gehenna.

Knowing this is the case, John falls on his face in humble adoration. "Then I fell at his feet to worship him. But he said to me, 'Do not do that; I am a fellow servant of yours and your brethren who hold the testimony of Jesus; worship God. For the testimony of Jesus is the spirit of prophecy'" (verse 10).

The angel rightly rebukes John. We do not worship angels nor do we worship fellow servants of Christ. We all have different gifts. We do not place creatures upon pedestals of adoration. Worship God! The testimony of Jesus is the Word of God concerning Christ, His life, death, and resurrection. The prophetic Word sets forth this testimony with life changing power.

The scene once again changes. We step back from the brink of judgment and the edge of the end of time. We see Jesus. He comes in power and splendor. Is this the second coming of Christ? Some think it is. I think the link is with the present age, the ongoing spread of the gospel, and the victory of Christ in Armageddon. See the exposition of Revelation 16:13-16. Christ rides forth to victory.

Gird Your sword on Your thigh, O Mighty One,
In Your splendor and Your majesty!
And in Your majesty ride on victoriously,
For the cause of truth and meekness and righteousness;
Let Your right hand teach You awesome things (Psalm 45:3-4).

Christ is presently fulfilling and will fulfill Psalm 45. John speaks, verse 11. "And I saw heaven opened, and behold, a white horse, and He who sat on it is called Faithful and True, and in righteousness He judges and wages war." Christ, the majestic King, is faithful to the Word of His Father (Hebrews 10:9). He wages successful spiritual warfare (John 18:36, 2 Corinthians 10:3-5). The following description displays His awesome visage.

Verse 12. "His eyes are a flame of fire, and on His head are many diadems; and He has a name written on Him which no one knows except Himself." Christ's vision is a searching flame (Revelation 1:14). His many crowns symbolize His universal reign. His Name? He alone can plummet the depth of the knowledge of God. Christ is knowable but also incomprehensible. Verse 13 tells us this. "He is clothed with a robe dipped in blood, and His name is called The Word of God." In one breath John cannot know His Name. In the next breath John is told His name. The idea is that Christ's robe is spattered with the blood of His enemies. If dipped in blood it is the hem of the garment stained with blood.[58]

The church of Jesus Christ is an army. In this world it is militant. In the world to come the church is triumphant. Verse 14: "And the armies which are in heaven, clothed in fine linen, white and clean, were following Him on white horses." The white garments are the righteousness of Christ. The white horses symbolize victory.

Verse 15 continues the description of Christ. "From His mouth comes a sharp sword, so that with it He may strike down the nations, and He will rule them with a rod of iron and He treads the wine press of the fierce wrath of God, the Almighty." This Shepherd-Warrior implements Psalm 2. Christ fulfills the Great Commission. God the Father's promise to the Son is in Psalm 2:8-9.

> Ask of Me, and I will surely give the nations as Your inheritance,
> And the very ends of the earth as Your possession.
> You shall break them with a rod of iron.
> You shall shatter them like earthenware.

Compare Matthew 28:19 where Christ commands the disciples to take the gospel to "all the nations" and Acts 1:8 where He tells the disciples their witness will reach to the "remotest part of the earth." The sharp sword is the Word of God. The iron scepter is Christ's firm rule. No one falls from his hand. Christ subdues hearts and brings men and women under the sway of His power by His Word, the gospel. Where men and women do not submit, Christ will crush and shatter them in judgment like weak clay pots.

We therefore see another aspect of His person and character. Verse 16. "And on His robe and on His thigh He has a name written, 'KING OF KINGS, AND LORD OF LORDS.'" This Name not only reveals Christ's sovereignty, it is also the righteous counterpart of the unholy name with which Babylon is sealed. "BABYLON THE GREAT, THE MOTHER OF HARLOTS AND OF THE ABOMINATIONS OF THE EARTH" (Revelation 17:5).

As Christ rides to victory and the gospel pervades the nations, God is preparing the church for its wedding. The reprobate are running head-long toward another feast called the Great Supper of God. Perdition awaits. Verses 17-18:

> Then I saw an angel standing in the sun, and he cried out with a loud voice, saying to all the birds which fly in midheaven, "Come, assemble for the great

---

[58] The NASB reads, "a robe dipped in blood," from the original ἱμάτιν βεβαμμένον αἵματι. Perhaps "a robe having been baptized in blood." From this we may take the image to be a robe spattered with blood rather than dipped and soaked with blood.

supper of God, so that you may eat the flesh of kings and the flesh of commanders and the flesh of mighty men and the flesh of horses and of those who sit on them and the flesh of all men, both free men and slaves, and small and great."

The picture comes from Ezekiel 39:17-21 and the defeat of God's enemies. The wedding of Christ represents the joy and felicity of heaven. The Great Supper of God portrays judgment and the perpetual agony of hell. On one hand there is a feast of gladness. On the other hand there is a banquet of gloom and despair.

The angel takes his position in the sun. The message cannot be missed. The question is clear. To which feast are you headed? Are you engaged to Christ the King with a wedding soon to follow? Or are you among all the categories of earth, small and great, who glory in Babylon and await the doom associated with the Great Supper of God?

The Millennium

Revelation 19:19-20:4

Christ and his army are marching forward to victory (Revelation 19:11-16). At the same time, the hordes of Gog (Ezekiel 39:11), the unbelieving world, are also called together. Revelation 11:7, 16:13-16 and 20:8 are parallels to Revelation 19:19-21:

> And I saw the beast and the kings of the earth and their armies assembled to make war against Him who sat on the horse and against His army. And the beast was seized, and with him the false prophet who performed the signs in his presence, by which he deceived those who had received the mark of the beast and those who worshipped his image; these two were thrown alive into the lake of fire which burns with brimstone. And the rest were killed with the sword which came from the mouth of Him who sat on the horse, and all the birds were filled with their flesh.

This is Armageddon, *the* decisive spiritual battle pictured in all previous and lesser armageddons. This is the scene given in Psalm 2:1-3. The best course of action is to "kiss the Son" (Psalm 2:12). Christ is victor. In the vision, Christ seizes the beast and His companion, the false prophet. The lake of fire receives these unholy and ungodly institutions.

Of course, in reality, people compose these institutions. People consumed with the ideals of anti-Christian power worked out in government, education, science, the arts, and various forms of media are consumed in everlasting torment, the second death (Revelation 20:14). Babylon, the capitol of evil, was and is the home of the beast and false prophet. The mark of the beast is the unholy spirit animating those who follow the beast. Babylon is fallen. The beast and false prophet also fall.

The great supper of God concludes with the picture of Christ slaying evil with the sword from His mouth. The pronouncements of judgment in Scripture are as sure as the promises of blessing. The visions once again bring us to the end of time and to eternity.

Revelation 20 begins the seventh section containing Revelation 20, 21, and 22. As the previous section detailed the doom of Babylon, this final section of Revelation gives us a glimpse of the New Jerusalem. In Revelation we see two women, the harlot and the woman with child: two cities, Babylon and New Jerusalem; two destinies, heaven and hell. *In general*, Revelation 20-21 gives us the details of life in the New Jerusalem, the city of God.

Revelation 20 begins with an overview of this present age. Verses 1-2: "Then I saw an angel coming down from heaven, holding the key of the abyss and a great chain in his hand. And he laid hold of the dragon, the serpent of old, who is the devil and Satan, and bound him for a thousand years."

John sees another heavenly messenger. This one has a key. It is the key for the abyss first revealed in Revelation 9:2. This angel also has a chain. The key and chain are not literal but symbolic. The angel has the power to open the pit of hell.

The angel also has power to restrain the devil. This is power exercised on behalf of Christ who controls history. The dragon is the devil (Revelation 12:9). Christ, exercising His purpose, thus restrains the devil so gospel light may spread over the world and abate pagan darkness. The picture does not relate the complete inactivity of Satan. Verse 3 confirms this. "And he threw him into the abyss, and shut it and sealed it over him, so that he would not deceive the nations any longer, until the thousand years were completed; after these things he must be released for a short time."

Satan is restrained for a particular purpose, that he might not deceive the nations. The power of the devil to keep men and women in pagan darkness is broken. The gospel advances. Individuals from every tribe and tongue and people and nation may be converted. Only one nation had the Word of God at the time of Christ, Israel. Now that Word spans the globe. To this extent, Satan is bound.

The period of this binding is 1000 years. This is the only place in the Bible where the term millennium appears. The millennium is not a literal future age of 1000 years. The number 1000 is symbolic. The number 10 is the number of completeness or perfection with regard to earthly matters. Ten cubed is a large perfect number. It is the time during which God perfectly fulfills His purposes in this world. Paul tells us the same thing in Ephesians 1:9-10: "He made known to us the mystery of His will, according to His kind intention which He purposed in Him with a view to an administration suitable to the fullness of the times, that is the summing up of all things in Christ, things in the heavens and things on the earth."

God's scheme is to bring all of creation into subjection to Christ. The goal will be met at the end of time. The times and epochs will be filled with all the events prescribed by God. As God presently carries out His purposes, Christ is the administrator of this estate known as creation. God's administration through Christ is suitable to the goal of summing up all things in Christ. When the times and epochs are filled with the proper events, the 1000 years will be complete.

During this gospel period, Christ reigns as King. The basic confession of the church is, "Jesus is Lord." Romans 10:9, "If you confess with your mouth Jesus as Lord, and believe in your heart that God raised Him from the dead, you will be saved." The spread of the gospel is rooted in the Lordship of Christ. And Jesus came up and spoke to them, saying, "All authority has been given to Me in heaven and on earth. Go therefore and make disciples of all the nations."

Verse 4 introduces another view of this gospel period. "Then I saw thrones, and they sat on them, and judgment was given to them." Converted people have a privileged status. Jesus promises in Revelation 3:21, "He who overcomes, I will grant to him to sit down with Me on My throne." And Paul tells us part of our gospel privilege involves reigning with Christ. God, being rich in mercy, raised us up with Christ "and seated us with Him in the heavenly places"

151

(Ephesians 2:6). Our reign *with* Christ is affected as we faithfully proclaim his blessings and judgments. The millennium is now.

The First Resurrection

Revelation 20:4-15

Those who reign with Christ have been made alive with Christ. Again, Ephesians 2:4-5 speaks of this first and all-important spiritual resurrection. "But God, being rich in mercy, because of His great love with which He loved us, even when we were dead in our transgressions, made us alive together with Christ (by grace you have been saved)." Note that Paul logically places this spiritual resurrection before reigning with Christ.

We have a similar picture as we continue with Revelation 20:4:

> And I saw the souls of those who had been beheaded because of their testimony of Jesus and because of the word of God, and those who had not worshipped the beast or his image, and had not received the mark on their forehead and on their hand; and they came to life and reigned with Christ for a thousand years.

As in Revelation 6:9-11, the picture of martyrs represents all saints who witness for Christ. The word witness is the Greek word *martus*, martyr. This is not a select number of believers. These people do not carry the mark of the beast, the unholy spirit. They have the mark and seal of God, the fruit of the Holy Spirit (Ephesians 1:13-14, Galatians 5:22-23).

These people came to life and reigned with Christ. This *coming to life* is the first resurrection. Verse 5: "The rest of the dead did not come to life until the thousand years were completed. This is the first resurrection."

The parable of the prodigal son is significant here. The son returned to his father to beg forgiveness. When the son returned, the father exclaimed, "But we had to celebrate and rejoice, for this brother of yours was dead and has begun to live, and was lost and has been found" (Luke 15:32). The Authorized Version says the son was "alive again." Revelation 20:4 uses the same word to refer to the first resurrection.[59] It is a spiritual resurrection. It is the same resurrection mentioned by Paul in Ephesians 2:5. Verse 6 confirms this interpretation.

"Blessed and holy is the one who has a part in the first resurrection; over these the second death has no power, but they will be priests of God and of Christ and will reign with Him for a thousand years."

There is a first resurrection and a second resurrection. There is a first death and a second death. The first resurrection is spiritual. The second is physical. The first death is physical. The second death is spiritual. Verse 14 tells us the second death is the lake of fire. Individuals who are born again, who have come to life spiritually, need never fear they will have a part in the lake of fire. The second death has no power over them. They are priests of God. They reign with

---

[59] Luke 15:32 [NJKV], "is alive again" translates ἔζησεν Revelation 20:4 [NASB], "they came to life" translates ἔζησαν. The only difference between the two texts is the singular in Luke 15:32 and the plural in Revelation 20:4.

153

Christ. They participate in the present millennial reign of Christ. This is the case for us as we propagate the gospel and faithfully declare the Lordship of Christ to the nations. Christ uses His gospel to bring men and women under the sway of His power. Thus we participate in His millennial reign.

Verses 7-8 now tell us the millennium is not only a period of time. It is a state of affairs. "When the thousand years are completed, Satan will be released from his prison, and will come out to deceive the nations which are in the four corners of the earth, Gog and Magog, to gather them together for the war; the number of them is like the sand of the seashore."

We see here the millennium is a state of affairs. There is a sense in which Satan is bound. The visions portray this. There is also a sense in which Satan carries out his malicious intents within specific constraints. "Your adversary, the devil, prowls around like a roaring lion, seeking someone to devour" (1 Peter 5:8). Yet he is under orders. He cannot exceed the limits set by God (Job 1:12). Satan still does his dirty work. Outside the millennium, outside the kingdom of Christ, the devil still has a people. This is perpetually the case as God promised in the Garden. See Genesis 3:15. And so the devil gathers his forces for war against God's anointed (Psalm 2:1-3). This is the picture. The parallel passages are Revelation 11:7-10, 16:13-16, and 19:19.

The battle is engaged in verse 9. "And they came up on the broad plain of the earth and surrounded the camp of the saints and the beloved city, and fire came down from heaven and devoured them."

This is a vision, a picture, a portrayal of reality but not reality itself. We must continually remind ourselves of this. The battles are spiritual. They are difficult. The church, the city of God, is always under siege. The victory is the Lord's. "'Not by might nor by power, but by My Spirit,' says the Lord of hosts" (Zechariah 4:6). The fire of judgment consumes God's enemies. We must trust the Sovereign King to deliver us.

We have seen Babylon, the beast, and the false prophet each meet their doom. Verse 10 shows us the end of the devil. "And the devil who deceived them was thrown into the lake of fire and brimstone, where the beast and the false prophet are also; and they will be tormented day and night forever and ever."

Heaven is forever. Hell is eternal. The punishment for crimes against the infinitely holy God is *eternal* fire. With the demise of Satan comes the final assize.

Then I saw a great white throne and Him who sat upon it, from whose presence earth and heaven fled away, and no place was found for them. And I saw the dead, the great and the small, standing before the throne, and books were opened; and another book was opened, which is the book of life; and the dead were judged from the things which were written in the books, according to their deeds. And the sea gave up the dead which were in it, and death and Hades gave up the dead which were in them; and they were judged, every one of them according to their deeds (Verses 11-13).

Fear grips unbelievers. The ledgers of life reveal their evil deeds. There is no escape. Punishment comes because of sin.

"Then death and Hades were thrown into the lake of fire. This is the second death, the lake of fire. And if anyone's name was not found written in the book of life, he was thrown into the lake of fire (verses 14-15)."

Two points. "The last enemy that will be abolishe is death" (1 Corinthians 15:26). God is not a God of double jeopardy. Christ did *not* pay for the sins of those *not* written in the book of life. They must pay for their sins themselves.

The Church, The Bride, New Jerusalem

Revelation 21:1-14

Chapters 17-19 outline the fall and doom of Babylon. Chapters 20-22 detail the exaltation and glory of the church, the bride of Christ, New Jerusalem. Chapter 20 gives us a summary. Now the visions reveal the details. We also see New Jerusalem, the bride of Christ and glory of God, is an everlasting monument to the grace of God. Revelation 21:1-8 reveals New Jerusalem as the bride of Christ, the dwelling place of God, the fulfillment of the covenant of grace.

Verse 1: "Then I saw a new heaven and a new earth; for the first heaven and the first earth passed away, and there is no longer any sea." We see what it means to be *new* when we comprehend the *new* heart God gives in the *new* birth. "Therefore if anyone is in Christ, he is a *new* creature; the old things passed away; behold, *new* things have come" (2 Corinthians 5:17). This gift is the promise of the *new* covenant.

The *new* heart is given by God with the gift of the Holy Spirit. The *new* heart is a Spirit directed heart. By the power of the Spirit, we become *new* creatures. We are disposed to do *new* things, that which is outlined in God's Word. The new heavens and new earth are therefore the redeemed heaven and earth. The fallen, curse laden world is gone. The sea represents the world outside of Christ. It, too, is gone.

Verse 2: "And I saw the holy city, New Jerusalem, coming down out of heaven from God, made ready as a bride adorned for her husband." The New Jerusalem is the City of God. The source and power of the City of God is heaven. There is a sense in which New Jerusalem is *presently* coming down from heaven. This city is the bride of Christ. There is no division between Old Testament imagery and New Testament reality. There is continuity between the Old Testament people of God and the Church. The bride of Christ is *presently* being prepared for her wedding.

Verse 3: "And I heard a loud voice from the throne, saying, 'Behold, the tabernacle of God is among men, and He will dwell among them, and they shall be His people, and God Himself will be among them.'" Here we have the final and glorious fulfillment of the covenant of grace. This covenant involves our union and communion with the living God. The covenant is summed up in the words of Leviticus 26:12, "I will also walk among you and be your God, and you shall be My people." Christ fulfills these words. He is Immanuel, God with us (Matthew 1:23). The highest privilege in the visible church is coming to the communion table to partake of Christ by faith. Thus we confess and God confesses, "I am your God and you are my people." Revelation 21:3 brings a picture of consummate fulfillment.

Verse 4: "And He will wipe away every tear from their eyes; and there will no longer be any death; there will no longer be any mourning, or crying, or pain; the first things have passed away." This is a picture of the reversal of the curse. Death is the curse of sin. Disease is incipient death. At the consummation, death is no more. "O death, where is your victory? O death, where is your sting?" (1 Corinthians 15:55). All that leads to death disappears. There are therefore no more tears. There is unspeakable joy. "Old things passed away; behold, new things have come" (2 Corinthians 5:17).

Verse 5 confirms. "And He who sits on the throne said, 'Behold, I am making all things new.' And He said, 'Write, for these words are faithful and true.'" The words of the vision reflect the fact we are at the consummation. "Then He said to me, 'It is done. I am the Alpha and the Omega, the beginning and the end. I will give to the one who thirsts from the spring of the water of life without cost. He who overcomes will inherit these things, and I will be his God and he will be My son'" (verses 6-7). The beginning and the end are now known. Those thirsting for righteousness are satisfied. The covenant of grace is fulfilled in intimate fellowship with the Father.

Verse 8 again shows us the other side of the coin of justice and mercy. "But for the cowardly and unbelieving and abominable and murderers and immoral persons and sorcerers and idolaters and all liars, their part will be in the lake that burns with fire and brimstone, which is the second death." Death, eternal death, is the lot of all those outside of grace. This *second* death is eternal and spiritual.

The visions then emphasize New Jerusalem is the bride of Christ, the consummate church of both the Old and New Testaments. Verse 9: "Then one of the seven angels who had the seven bowls full of the seven last plagues came and spoke with me, saying, 'Come here, I will show you the bride, the wife of the Lamb.'" Compare Revelation 17:1. One of the seven angels took John, in the Spirit, into the wilderness to see the doom of Babylon. Now an angel takes John to a vantage point where he can see the glorious bride of Christ. Again, this bride is New Jerusalem coming out of heaven. The glory of God fills the city. Verses 10-11: "And he carried me away in the Spirit to a great and high mountain, and showed me the holy city, Jerusalem, coming down out of heaven from God, having the glory of God. Her brilliance was like a very costly stone, as a stone of crystal-clear jasper."

Verses 12-14 give further descriptions and the number twelve is prominent as in Revelation 7:4-8.

> It had a great and high wall, with twelve gates, and at the gates twelve angels; and names were written on them, which are the names of the twelve tribes of the sons of Israel. There were three gates on the east and three gates on the north and three gates on the south and three gates on the west. And the wall of the city had twelve foundation stones, and on them were the twelve names of the twelve apostles of the Lamb (Revelation 21:12-14).

The twelve gates and twelve foundation stones picture the continuity between the Old and New Testaments. We also have a picture of the church built on the foundation of the Old Testament prophets and New Testament apostles (Ephesians 2:20).

God's Memorial, New Jerusalem

Revelation 21:15-27

New Jerusalem not only fulfills the covenant of grace, she is the pattern for both Old Testament tabernacle and temple. See Hebrews 8:4-5.

Verse 15: "The one who spoke with me had a gold measuring rod to measure the city, and its gates and its wall." The rod used to measure the church is the Word of God. It is the gold standard. Refer back to a similar picture in Revelation 11:1ff. Every member of the city as well as all prophets and apostles are measured against this gold standard.

Verse 16: "The city is laid out as a square, and its length is as great as the width; and he measured the city with the rod, fifteen hundred miles; its length and width and height are equal." The city is cubical as was the Holy of Holies in the tabernacle in the wilderness and the temple in Jerusalem. The Holy of Holies was the special place where God met with Moses. The church is the special dwelling place of God in the world. New Jerusalem is the consummate dwelling place of God. The measurement is twelve thousand stadia. The number *twelve* again refers to the church. The cube is symbolic of perfection. The number *one thousand* is a large number of perfect wholeness. This is the church of God perfected by Christ.

Verse 17: "And he measured its wall, seventy-two yards, according to human measurements, which are also angelic measurements." Again, the English translation does not preserve the symbolism. The wall is one hundred forty-four cubits high, twelve squared. The wall is low compared to the height of the city, symbolically easy to cross. The material of the wall and city is unusual to say the least. "The material of the wall was jasper; and the city was pure gold, like clear glass" (verse 18).

Revelation 4:3 describes God as jasper-like. "And He who was sitting was like a jasper stone and a sardius in appearance." The City of God would therefore be like her Master. We saw this in verse 11. New Jerusalem has "the glory of God. Her brilliance was like a very costly stone, as a stone of crystal-clear jasper." And so the wall of the city, the church, displays the glory of God. Of necessity, this must be the case in heaven and should be the case on earth. The city is pure gold but also transparent. The Christian life is of great value. Transparency is also a virtue of life in Christ.

The foundation stones, the twelve apostles, are also represented as costly building blocks. Verses 19-20:

> The foundation stones of the city wall were adorned with every kind of precious stone. The first foundation stone was jasper; the second, sapphire; the third, chalcedony; the fourth, emerald; the fifth, sardonyx; the sixth, sardius; the seventh, chrysolite; the eighth, beryl; the ninth, topaz; the tenth, chrysoprase; the eleventh, jacinth; the twelfth, amethyst.

The teachings of the apostles and prophets are of supreme value to the church. "They are more desirable than gold, yes, than much fine gold; sweeter also than honey and the drippings of the honeycomb" (Psalm 119:10). As we follow these teachings and build upon them, we are prepared for the coming of Christ and the wedding of the Lamb.

Verse 21: "And the twelve gates were twelve pearls; each one of the gates was a single pearl. And the street of the city was pure gold, like transparent glass." We recall the parable of the pearl of great price, Matthew 13:45-46. "Again, the kingdom of heaven is like a merchant seeking fine pearls, and upon finding one pearl of great value, he went and sold all that he had and bought it." Gaining entrance into the celestial city is worth everything. Jesus also puts it in the negative, asking a pointed question. "For what will it profit a man if he gains the whole world and forfeits his soul?" (Matthew 16:26).

We just saw the City of God radiates the glory of God. The following verses expand this picture. Verses 22-23: "I saw no temple in it, for the Lord God the Almighty and the Lamb are its temple. And the city has no need of the sun or of the moon to shine on it, for the glory of God has illumined it, and its lamp is the Lamb." God is our sanctuary, our hiding place, our refuge. Psalm 18:2 uses similar language. "The Lord is my rock and my fortress and my deliverer, my God, my rock, in whom I take refuge; my shield and the horn of my salvation, my stronghold."

God is also the light of the city. The sun and moon provide light and life. They point to the light and life of God. "The nations will walk by its light, and the kings of the earth will bring their glory into it" (verse 24). As all nations receive light from the *sun*, all nations will receive light from the *Son*. Every tribe, tongue, people, and nation is represented in the church.

Verses 25-26: "In the daytime (for there will be no night there) its gates will never be closed; and they will bring the glory and the honor of the nations into it." Night—darkness—is the time of evil and the picture of corruption. There is no night, no darkness, in New Jerusalem. Walled cities closed their gates at night for protection. No such measures are needed in the City of God.

Verse 27: "And nothing unclean, and no one who practices abomination and lying, shall ever come into it, but only those whose names are written in the Lamb's book of life." Sinners may not be excluded from the visible church in this world. They are banished from the church triumphant in heaven. Only those whose names are in the book of life from eternity past are citizens of New Jerusalem. They give praise to God for His rich grace. "Blessed be the God and Father of our Lord Jesus Christ, who has blessed us with every spiritual blessing in the heavenly places in Christ, just as He chose us in Him before the foundation of the world (Ephesians 1:3-4)."

As the smoke of her burning rises eternally over Babylon, forever signaling the wrath of God against sin, so the songs of Zion will ever rise above Jerusalem's walls. Babylon's judgment is an eternal monument to God's justice. New Jerusalem forever calls to mind the mercy and grace of God. New

Jerusalem is therefore an everlasting monument to God's grace. New Jerusalem reflects the glory of God and the majesty of Christ. Glory be to His great Name.

Keep the Words of this Prophecy

Revelation 22:1-9

The great theme of Revelation is the glory of God and majesty of Christ. Revelation 22 now urges us to keep the words of the prophecy of this book. We do so as we recognize the sovereign God of the universe and realize we are part of His story.

Chapter 22 continues the description of New Jerusalem, the bride of Christ. It is the location of the river of life, the tree of life, and the light of life. Verse 1: "Then he showed me a river of the water of life, clear as crystal, coming from the throne of God and of the Lamb in the middle of its street."

The water of life, the Holy Spirit, flows from the throne of the Father *and* the Son. Compare John 4:14, Revelation 7:17 and 21:6. We must drink of this water to live. Here again we see the Father and the Son equated. The divinity of Jesus Christ shines. Verse 2 describes the river leading from the throne. "On either side of the river was the tree of life, bearing twelve kinds of fruit, yielding its fruit every month; and the leaves of the tree were for the healing of the nations."

The picture is difficult. The river of the water of life flows down the middle of a great street leading from the throne. The word *tree*, perhaps a synecdoche, may be used collectively to represent twelve trees. They line the river. They bear twelve differing fruits. Here the nations find healing. This is a picture. It is symbolism, a picture of reality and not reality itself. We do not have here a specific ground for herbal remedies.

After the fall, God cast Adam out of the garden away from the tree of life. "So He drove the man out; and at the east of the garden of Eden He stationed the cherubim and the flaming sword which turned every direction to guard the way to the tree of life" (Genesis 3:24). Citizens of New Jerusalem have free access to the tree(s) of life. Revelation 2:7 reminds us, "To him who overcomes, I will grant to eat of the tree of life which is in the Paradise of God." First John 5:4 explains: "For whatever is born of God overcomes the world; and this is the victory that has overcome the world, our faith. Who is the one who overcomes the world, but he who believes that Jesus is the Son of God?" We overcome through faith in the victorious gospel (Revelation 6:1-2), by trusting the One who always rides to victory (Revelation 19:11-16).

Verse 3: "There will no longer be any curse; and the throne of God and of the Lamb will be in it, and His bond-servants will serve Him." Christ is God. He occupies one throne with the Father. The curse due to sin is no more. It involved separation from the love and mercy of God and exposure to the wrath and judgment of God. This was symbolized in Adam's ejection from Eden. Adam could no longer walk with God in the cool of the garden (Genesis 3:8). Now, citizens of New Jerusalem dwell securely *with* God and *with* Christ.

Verse 4 explains this fellowship of the citizens of heaven with the Father, "They will see His face, and His name will be on their foreheads." This is the beatific vision. Aaron foreshadowed it in his benediction.

The Lord bless you, and keep you;
The Lord make His face shine on you,
And be gracious to you;
The Lord lift up His countenance on you,
And give you peace (Numbers 6:24-26).

Note the repeated prayer of Psalm 80:3, 7, and 19. "O God, restore us and cause Your face to shine upon us, and we will be saved." The answer awaits those trusting Christ. "Beloved, now we are children of God, and it has not appeared as yet what we will be. We know that when He appears, we will be like Him, because we will see Him just as He is" (1 John 3:2). The name of God is His character filling the lives of His people. This is the mark of God. It is the ultimate blessing, His life shining through our lives.

Verse 5: "And there will no longer be any night; and they will not have need of the light of a lamp nor the light of the sun, because the Lord God will illumine them; and they will reign forever and ever." Through the vision we see how the light of God permeates the City of God. The illuminating power of God floods every life. The light of God's countenance fully awakens every soul. The people of God reign as they know God and implement His will. God's light comes in the form of knowledge and ability. We experience ultimate blessing as we implement God's Word by the power of His Spirit. This is the message.

Verses 6-7: "And he said to me, 'These words are faithful and true;' and the Lord, the God of the spirits of the prophets, sent His angel to show to His bond-servants the things which must soon take place. 'And behold, I am coming quickly. Blessed is he who heeds the words of the prophecy of this book.'"

The angel speaking to John indicates the truth and faithfulness of the visions. They are meant to portray events in heaven and on earth. Everything comes about in accordance with God's plans (Ephesians 1:11). Not only so, everything occurs that God might receive the glory due His Name (Ephesians 1:6, 12, and 14). The events in the Great Book (Revelation 5) unfold rapidly. We know this full well when we look *back* on our lives. This is the symbolic meaning of Jesus coming quickly.

How do we heed the words of the prophecy of this book? We see the majesty of God and of Christ. We realize history is His-story played out according to His purposes. We understand we are caught up in God's purposes (verses 6-7), not as pawns, but as servants. We therefore glory in God and in His Christ. These thoughts overwhelm John.

Verse 8: "I, John, am the one who heard and saw these things. And when I heard and saw, I fell down to worship at the feet of the angel who showed me these things." John falls on his face before the angel who was showing him the majesty, might, power, and glory of Christ. The response of the angel is immediate. "But he said to me, 'Do not do that. I am a fellow servant of yours and of your brethren the prophets and of those who heed the words of this book. Worship God'" (verse 9).

This is the whole point. We keep the words of the prophecy of this book. How? We recognize His Majesty. We worship God alone through Jesus Christ alone.

The Book is Open, Come

Revelation 22:10-21

Revelation 22 emphasizes the words of the prophecy of this book are open for all to read. They set before us life and death.

Verse 10: "And he said to me, 'Do not seal up the words of the prophecy of this book, for the time is near.'" The angel speaking to John directs him to publish the prophecy for the edification and encouragement of the church. The opposite was true for Daniel. "But as for you, Daniel, conceal these words and seal up the book until the end of time" (Daniel 12:4). "Go your way, Daniel, for these words are concealed and sealed up until the end time" (Daniel 12:9). We are the people upon whom the ends of the ages have come (1 Corinthians 10:11). It is the last time (1 Peter 1:20). The angel continues.

Verse 11: "Let the one who does wrong, still do wrong; and the one who is filthy, still be filthy; and let the one who is righteous, still practice righteousness; and the one who is holy, still keep himself holy."

There are notes of blessed and frightful determinism in these words. Both the righteous and the wicked will exist through eternity. This was God's pledge to the devil in Genesis 3:15. "I will put enmity between you and the woman, and between your seed and her seed." There will always be the elect and the reprobate, the seed of the woman and the seed of the serpent. They are New Jerusalem and Babylon respectively.

The greatest question we must ever answer concerns the city in which we reside. Are we numbered among the elect of God? Are we citizens of heaven? The only way to answer this question is to come to Christ and to persevere in Christ. "Therefore, brethren, be all the more diligent to make certain about His calling and choosing you" (2 Peter 1:10). The time will come when all is confirmed. The doors to the wedding feast will be closed. No one else will enter. We must therefore heed the words of the prophecy of this book.

Verse 12: "Behold, I am coming quickly, and My reward is with Me, to render to every man according to what he has done." We will spend eternity in either Babylon or New Jerusalem. Time is short.

Verse 13: "I am the Alpha and the Omega, the first and the last, the beginning and the end." Compare Revelation 1:8 and 21:6 where God the Father is the Alpha and the Omega. Christ is God. When we stand before Christ, we stand before God. When Christ passes judgment or extends mercy, God extends judgment or extends mercy.

Verse 14 pronounces a blessing. "Blessed are those who wash their robes, so that they may have the right to the tree of life, and may enter by the gates into the city." This is the seventh of the beatitudes in Revelation. I'll review them in the next lesson. They lay before us the perfect blessing of God. The robes, or clothes, represent our lives. Our own clothes are imperfect. "All of us have become like one who is unclean, and all our righteous deeds are like a filthy garment" (Isaiah 64:6). Our robes must be washed in the blood of Christ. Once cleared of guilt and cleansed from sin we have access to New Jerusalem and the tree of life.

The reprobate are outside the city. God does not grant them entrance. Verse 15: "Outside are the dogs and the sorcerers and the immoral persons and the murderers and the idolaters, and everyone who loves and practices lying." Lying is mentioned last. It is in the prominent position. The devil is a liar and the father of lies (John 8:44). "Those who practice such things will not inherit the kingdom of God" (Galatians 5:21).

Christ again speaks. He uses the mediation of angels. Verse 16: "I, Jesus, have sent My angel to testify to you these things for the churches. I am the root and the descendant of David, the bright morning star." The messages given to John are open. They are for the churches. Take heed to the words of the prophecy of this book. The speaker authenticates Himself. Christ is *the* descendent of David. Compare Revelation 5:5 and Isaiah 11:1 and 10. Christ is the morning star. Compare Numbers 24:17 and 2 Peter 1:19.

Verse 17: "The Spirit and the bride say, 'Come.' And let the one who hears say, 'Come.' And let the one who is thirsty come; let the one who wishes take the water of life without cost." The words of the seemingly enigmatic visions become clear. Since the doom of Babylon is sure and the exaltation of New Jerusalem is without parallel, come to Christ. The message of the bride is the message of the Spirit. Come. Those who are willing may take of the water of life freely. Remember verse 11. Humanity is divided between willing and *un*willing.

Verse 18 issues a warning. Do not add or subtract from the words of the prophecy of this book. "I testify to everyone who hears the words of the prophecy of this book: if anyone adds to them, God will add to him the plagues which are written in this book." Compare Deuteronomy 4:2: "You shall not add to the word which I am commanding you, nor take away from it, that you may keep the commandments of the Lord your God which I command you."

You cannot add or take away from the words of this prophecy and get the message. You cannot add or take away from the prophecy of this book and keep the words. Pun intended. Failure to heed is disastrous.

Verse 19: "And if anyone takes away from the words of the book of this prophecy, God will take away his part from the tree of life and from the holy city, which are written in this book." Those who alter the book to suit their whims remain unwilling to come to Christ. They hunger for unrighteousness. They will never be satisfied. Matthew 5:6 relates the opposite. "Blessed are those who hunger and thirst for righteousness, for they shall be satisfied." Those who hunger for unrighteousness will have their way. They will choke eternally on smoke-filled judgments as a part of doomed Babylon.

Verses 20-21 conclude the book. "He who testifies to these things says, 'Yes, I am coming quickly.' Amen. Come, Lord Jesus. The grace of the Lord Jesus be with all. Amen." Jesus is Lord. The majesty of Christ is preeminent. History unfolds rapidly. We cannot hold it back. Why? It is God's story. Christ is unfolding it. As said above, when we look *back*, we see how quickly time passes. Recognize the majesty of Christ. Realize you are part of His-story. The book is open. Come.

Perfect Blessedness: Seven Beatitudes

Part One

When I pointed out to my congregation there are *seven* beatitudes in the marvelous book of Revelation, there was immediate interest. In another context, a good friend said, "I want to see what you do with them."

We find beatitudes throughout Scripture, especially in the Psalter. Psalm 1:1 counsels, "Blessed is the man who does not walk in the counsel of the wicked, nor stand in the path of sinners, nor sit in the seat of scoffers." The Psalms teach us the blessings of life with and before God. Psalm 2 reminds us we ought to flee to Christ. "Blessed are all who take refuge in Him" (verse 12). There are twenty-six of these beatitudes in the Psalter.

Since Revelation leans upon Old Testament themes and pictures, we should not be surprised to find several beatitudes in this book. *Seven* comes to the fore immediately. It is the number of perfection or completion. Revelation represents the church universal with seven churches (1:11). There are seven lampstands and seven stars.

"As for the mystery of the seven stars which you saw in My right hand, and the seven golden lampstands: the seven stars are the angels of the seven churches, and the seven lampstands are the seven churches" (1:20).

God commissions messengers, pastors. He places them in churches to proclaim the perfect light of heaven. The church is the light of God in the world. Revelation 3:1 speaks of the seven Spirits of God. God's Holy Spirit is perfection.

Now we see *seven* beatitudes. The word blessed or happy is the same word used in the Greek version of the Old Testament and the same word we find in the beatitudes of Matthew 5. Blessed, happy, is the one . . . This is not a joy born of earthly pleasure. It is a joy we derive from heaven, from God, only through Jesus Christ. It is a perfect happiness, a perfect blessedness. As a result, I say we are perfectly blessed as we grasp the significance of the seven beatitudes of Revelation and fully act on them.

The first beatitude comes in the introduction of the book. "Blessed is he who reads and those who hear the words of the prophecy, and heed the things which are written in it" (1:3). This is the overarching theme. To grasp the blessing we must understand the prophecy of Revelation. Those of you who have followed my exposition of the book will recall the primary theme of Christ's majesty. Revelation calls us to come to grips with the glory, greatness, and majesty of Christ, God manifest to us, with us and in us. We take heed to the prophecy of this book when we recognize the sovereign God of the universe and realize we are part of His-story. Ultimate happiness comes when we bow before the Christ who unfolds this history. The tone is set with this beatitude.

My exposition of Revelation follows the recapitulation approach to the book. There are seven cycles in this book. Revelation reviews the period from the first advent to the second coming of Christ seven times from varying perspectives. In each cycle, the visions fill in this period of time with ever increasing detail. The visions also shift from emphasis on the early part of the period to the end. Finally, there is increasing emphasis upon the heavenly glory awaiting the saints and the terrible doom prepared for the reprobate. In keeping with this overall viewpoint, the beatitudes of Revelation fall toward the end of sections and for the most part toward the end of the book in the final section. This, I think, emphasizes the heavenly aspect of the hope to which God calls the elect and the eternal doom awaiting those outside of Christ.

The second beatitude is in Revelation 14:13 toward the close of section four encompassing chapters 12-14. "Blessed are the dead who die in the Lord from now on." This section details the warfare between the dragon inspired beast and the people of God. Special blessing comes to those who die in the Lord. They die trusting Christ. They have ultimate happiness. The words *from now on* may refer to the special blessing which comes to believers at death.

We note two things. This beatitude consoles us in the midst of battle and struggle. It tells us the victory belongs to Christ. We may die and pass from this life in the midst of battle. Yet we have great hope as we persevere in the faith. In addition, the beatitude directly reminds us that eternal verities take priority over earthly values.

The third beatitude takes us to the end of the next section of the book. Chapters 15 and 16 lay before us an awesome view of judgment, the seven bowls of wrath. "Blessed is the one who stays awake and keeps his clothes, so that he will not walk about naked and men will not see his shame" (16:15). The beatitude reminds us of the need to persevere in the faith if we are going to die in the Lord.

Perseverance requires vigilance. We must stay awake spiritually. Deception comes easily. The immediate context of this beatitude is Armageddon. This battle represents titanic spiritual warfare. We all have our Armageddons. They are decisive spiritual battles that change the course of our lives. In the midst of these significant battles we must keep our spiritual wits about us.

We must be mindful of our need of Christ. Only His righteousness, His garments, suffice as we stand before God. Without Christ's righteousness, we are without hope. We are naked. Without Christ's righteousness we will suffer ultimate shame. With it we have the hope of the resurrection. We have ultimate happiness before God. We join the ranks of heaven to give praise around the throne.

And so beatitude four reminds us, "Blessed are those who are invited to the marriage supper of the Lamb" (19:9). This beatitude comes toward the end of the sixth section of Revelation. Chapters 17 through 19 detail the fall and judgment of Babylon. Babylon is the capital of evil. She is the opposite of New Jerusalem, the center of holiness.

Christ came into this world as a bridegroom. The church is now in an engagement period. Christ will return for His bride. The stage is being set for the wedding. Those who trust Christ, heed His Word and persevere, are invited to the wedding of the lamb. This is the greatest invitation a person can ever receive.

Part Two

Recall that beatitude one sets the tone for our discussion. We must heed the prophecy of the book of Revelation. We do so by recognizing the majesty of Christ. We trust the Christ of God who is the King of history. We persevere in *the* faith made *our* faith by the sovereign God. We realize our privilege in receiving an invitation to the great Wedding Feast of the Lamb. We are blessed.

Since Revelation has seven sections, it is a perfect and complete review of the history of the New Testament church. Beatitudes two, three, and four come toward the end of sections four, five, and six respectively. Coming as they do *at the end of these sections*, these beatitudes confirm the recapitulation approach to the book I have been taking.

Beatitudes five, six, and seven are in the final section of the book. This, too, is in keeping with the overall scheme of Revelation. As the last sections of the book deal with our spiritual conflict, the demise of the beast, and the judgment of Babylon, they also hold forth our faith, our perseverance, and our hope as given in three beatitudes.

The last section of Revelation, chapters 20-22, emphasizes the final consummation and blessing of believers. Everything leads to this. Three of the beatitudes are in this final section to emphasize this final blessing. As the trend in the book is to emphasize final glory, so also the beatitudes. This, too, seems to me to confirm the seven fold recapitulation approach of interpretation.

Revelation 20:6, "Blessed and holy is the one who has a part in the first resurrection; over these the second death has no power." We determined the first resurrection is spiritual resurrection, new birth, or regeneration (Ephesians 2:5). The first death is physical death. The second death is spiritual, eternal torment, the lake of fire (Revelation 20:14). The second resurrection is therefore physical resurrection. Those who are born again, are blessed in a twofold way. New birth brings new life which issues in the resurrection of the body. This person is also holy, not innately so, but by virtue of union with Christ.

Here we see the progression of the beatitudes. First, there is the blessedness of trusting Christ so as to look forward to death in Christ. Second, there is the blessedness of perseverance in the faith, Christ with us in the midst of battle and spiritual conflict. Third, there is the blessedness of having the invitation to the wedding feast, of being people marked out by God for consummate communion with Christ. Then the wedding comes, "Blessed and holy is the one who has a part in the first resurrection; over these the second death has no power." "This is the second death, the lake of fire. If anyone's name was not found written in the book of life, he was thrown into the lake of fire" (Revelation 20:14-15). Christ comes to claim His bride, the church. The dead are raised incorruptible. "Thus we shall always be with the Lord. Therefore comfort one another with these words" (1 Thessalonians 4:17-18). We are truly blessed.

In this way the beatitudes bring us to the culmination of earthly history. This is not the end of the story however. We learn by repetition. God constructed us in this way. The sevenfold repetition of Revelation reminds us of this. The beatitudes also repeat the refrain. The conclusion of the book reminds us of the primary purpose with which we began. "Blessed is he who heeds the words of the prophecy of this book" (22:7). Compare Revelation 1:3, "Blessed is he who reads and those who hear the words of the prophecy, and heed the things which are written in it; for the time is near."

As already said several times, we heed the prophecy of this book by recognizing the majesty, power, and grace of God, coming before Him through Christ, the King of history, and bowing before His Majesty. This means our focus in faith and perseverance is preparation for the wedding.

Abraham sent his servant on a mission to procure a wife for his son, Isaac (Genesis 24). The servant took an oath to perform this duty. He went to Abraham's homeland. There, guided by God's angel, he met Rebekah. The servant gave Rebekah gifts from father Abraham. He returned with her to present her to son Isaac as his bride.

Every pastor, elder, and deacon in the church of Jesus Christ is a sworn servant of the Father. We are commissioned to enter the world to procure a bride for the Son. We bear the precious gift of the Father, the gospel. Our mission is to prepare the bride for Christ.

Much effort and planning goes into planning a wedding. It can be a daunting and exhausting task for the parents of the bride and for the bride herself. This is but a small picture of the overwhelming task of preparing for the wedding feast of Christ. If earthly weddings are a blessing, the Wedding Feast of the Lamb is ultimate joy and happiness. It is worthy of our life-long focus and attention. We take heed to the prophecy of the Book of Revelation if we understand the preeminence of this blessing and prepare for it.

As beatitude six takes us back to the beginning of Revelation, beatitude seven at once takes us back to the beginning of the Bible, to Genesis, and forward to the beatific vision in heaven. "Blessed are those who wash their robes, so that they may have the right to the tree of life, and may enter by the gates into the city" (22:14).

Those who wash their robes are sinners who mourn their lost condition and come to Christ to receive His righteousness. It is only clothed in Christ's righteousness that we may come to the tree of life and eat. Here, our saved, cleansed, and sanctified condition is confirmed for eternity. Adam and Eve were barred from the tree of life because of their sin. The saved of Christ have free access to the Garden of Glory and the tree of everlasting felicity.

The city is New Jerusalem, the glorious dwelling place of God. Those wearing the pristine robes of Christ's righteousness enter by the gate of Christ into The City. They are the sheep of God. They find their comfort, peace, and rest in God's presence. Restoration is accomplished. Reunion and communion with God through Christ is complete. The battles are over. The book of history is open. The trumpets have sounded. The vials are poured out. We are perfectly blessed in the full enjoying of God to all eternity (WSC, Answer 38).

The Time is Near

Input from Deuteronomy 32:35

An argument against a late date for the Book of Revelation and against the position I've taken with regard to both dating and the structure of Revelation comes from the very first verse of the book, Revelation 1:1. I've added the italics. "The Revelation of Jesus Christ, which God gave Him to show to His bond-servants, the things which *must soon take place*." If the things related in Revelation "must soon take place," from a strictly chronological perspective, then we must indeed insist upon an early date for the book, a date prior to 70 A.D. The Greek, ἐν τάχει, carries the force of *with speed, quickly, without delay.*

Revelation 1:3 presents a similar picture. Once again I've added the italics. "Blessed is he who reads and those who hear the words of the prophecy, and heed the things which are written in it; *for the time is near*." The Greek here reads, ὁ γὰρ καιρὸς ἐγγύς. Near refers to *being close* or *on the verge*.

The book closes with similar language. Revelation 22:6, with italics added, reads, "And he said to me, 'These words are faithful and true'; and the Lord, the God of the spirits of the prophets, sent His angel to show to His bond-servants the things which *must soon take place*." Revelation 22:10, again with italics added: "And he said to me, 'Do not seal up the words of the prophecy of this book, *for the time is near*.'" The Greek here is similar to Revelation 1:3, ὁ καιρὸς γὰρ ἐγγύς ἐστιν.

Kenneth Gentry calls these references "the time-texts [which are] the key to opening the door of Revelation."[60] Surely these texts militate against a Philosophy of History view of Revelation and push us into the Preterist position.

However, I suggest that the biblical data takes us in another direction. The imagery and message of Revelation rests on the Old Testament. Beale and McDonough note, "No other book of the NT is as permeated by the OT as Revelation."[61] They add, "It is generally recognized that Revelation contains more OT references than does any other NT book . . ."[62] And, "John leaves almost no OT stone unturned in the course of Revelation . . ."[63]

If this is the case, the language of Revelation 1:1, 1:3, 22:6, and 22:10 finds its roots in the Old Testament. In Deuteronomy 32, Moses gives Israel a great eschatological song. Verse 35 reads as follows: "Vengeance is Mine, and retribution, In due time their foot will slip; For the day of their calamity is near, And the impending things are hastening upon them." Moses clearly speaks of an

---

[60] Kenneth Gentry, *He Shall Have Dominion* (Tyler, TX: Institute for Christian Economics, 1992), 164.

[61] *Commentary on the New Testament Use of the Old Testament*, G.K. Beale and D.A. Carson, Editors (Grand Rapids: Baker, 2007), 1081.

[62] *Ibid.*, 1082.

[63] *Ibid.*

impending calamity which is *near* and is *hastening*. To grasp the import of the terminology of Deuteronomy 32:35, we examine this song of Moses.

We recall the people of God are in Moab prepared to cross the Jordan and enter the Promised Land. God commissions Moses to write this song and teach it to the people.

> Now therefore, write this song for yourselves, and teach it to the sons of Israel; put it on their lips, so that this song may be a witness for Me against the sons of Israel. For when I bring them into the land flowing with milk and honey, which I swore to their fathers, and they have eaten and are satisfied and become prosperous, then they will turn to other gods and serve them, and spurn Me and break My covenant. Then it shall come about, when many evils and troubles have come upon them, that this song will testify before them as a witness (for it shall not be forgotten from the lips of their descendants); for I know their intent which they are developing today, before I have brought them into the land which I swore (Deuteronomy 31:19-21).

God looks ahead and gives the people His prophetic word in the form of a song. The song, therefore, provides us with and Old Testament eschatology. "It contains the main themes of prophecy."[64] George Guthrie, leaning on Christensen's *Word Biblical Commentary*, indicates, "The song has three main movements. The first concerns the blessing of God on the people (32:1-14), the second addresses Israel's provocation of God's anger by their sin (32:15-29), and the third proclaims God's judgment and salvation (32:30-43) . . . "[65] Our text appears in the third section regarding God's judgment and salvation.

The uses of Moses' song in the New Testament validate it is prophetic and eschatological. After God delivers the people (vs. 6), carries them through the wilderness (vs. 10-12), and takes them into the Promised Land (vs. 13-14), the people turn their back on God (vs. 15-18). "They made Him jealous with strange *gods*; With abominations they provoked Him to anger" (vs. 16). Israel experienced a temporary and partial hardening. Paul says "a partial hardening happened to Israel until the fullness of the Gentiles has come in" (Romans 11:25).

Wrestling with the status of ethnic Israel, the apostle Paul quotes Deuteronomy 32:21. "So I will make them jealous with *those who* are not a people; I will provoke them to anger with a foolish nation."[66] It is Paul's judgment that this is the situation he faces. He so states in Romans 11:13-14, "But I am speaking to you who are Gentiles. Inasmuch then as I am an apostle of Gentiles, I magnify my ministry, if somehow I might move to jealousy my fellow countrymen and save some of them." God's provocation to anger and His jealousy result in His working to make Israel jealous with those who are "*not a*

---

[64] J. Ridderbos, *Deuteronomy* (Grand Rapids: Zondervan, 1984), 280.

[65] Op. cit., 931.

[66] See Romans 10:19.

people."[67] Paul views this as part of his ministry to the Gentiles. In other words, Moses appears to be looking forward centuries into the New Testament era. His song is eschatological.

Paul has already spoken of the Gentiles using this same language and referencing the prophet Hosea.

> What if God, although willing to demonstrate His wrath and to make His power known, endured with much patience vessels of wrath prepared for destruction? And *He did so* to make known the riches of His glory upon vessels of mercy, which He prepared beforehand for glory, *even* us, whom He also called, not from among Jews only, but also from among Gentiles. As He says also in Hosea, "I WILL CALL THOSE WHO WERE NOT MY PEOPLE, 'MY PEOPLE,' AND HER WHO WAS NOT BELOVED, 'BELOVED.' AND IT SHALL BE THAT IN THE PLACE WHERE IT WAS SAID TO THEM, 'YOU ARE NOT MY PEOPLE,' THERE THEY SHALL BE CALLED SONS OF THE LIVING GOD" (Romans 9:22-26).[68]

Moses language in Deuteronomy 32:21 refers to the Gentiles. Paul interprets this language as referring to the inclusion of the Gentiles in the New Testament era through the preaching of the Gospel. Paul also refers to Deuteronomy 32:43 in Romans 15. Deuteronomy 32:43 reads, "Rejoice, O nations, *with* His people." Paul once again connects the Song of Moses to his ministry to the Gentiles.

> For I say that Christ has become a servant to the circumcision on behalf of the truth of God to confirm the promises *given* to the fathers, and for the Gentiles to glorify God for His mercy; as it is written, "THEREFORE I WILL GIVE PRAISE TO YOU AMONG THE GENTILES, AND I WILL SING TO YOUR NAME." Again he says, "REJOICE, O GENTILES WITH HIS PEOPLE" (Romans 15:8-10).

In both these cases, Paul affirms the Song of Moses is both prophetic and eschatological.

This brings us to Deuteronomy 32:35-36.

> Vengeance is Mine, and retribution, In due time their foot will slip; For the day of their calamity is near, And the impending things are hastening upon them. For the LORD will vindicate His people, And will have compassion on His servants, When He sees that *their* strength is gone, And there is none *remaining*, bond or free.

Hebrews 10:30 picks up the first clause of both verse 35 and 36.

> The two utterances cited by our author come from the Song of Moses, the farewell address to the people of Israel in which their aged leader reminds them of God's gracious dealings with them and admonishes them regarding the dire

---

[67] Italics added. The Hebrew is simply בְלֹא־עָם.
[68] The Hebrew of Hosea 1:10 and 2:23 is לֹא־עַמִּי .

174

consequences of ingratitude and apostasy. Of the two declarations, the first, "Vengeance is mine, I will repay" (Dt. 32:35), applies both to the enemy from outside who refuses to acknowledge Yahweh's sway over him and the enemy from within the community of the covenant who rebels against the God he previously had professed to honor; while the second, "The Lord will judge His people" (Dt. 32:36), speaks as originally uttered, of judgment in the sense of vindication (cf. Ps. 135:14)—but, again, those with reference to whom the Lord's people are vindicated are not only alien adversaries but also the ones who contemptuously desert the fellowship of grace.[69]

In other words, judgment is coming. This judgment encompasses those within and those without the church. In this judgment, the true people of God will be vindicated. "[T]he character of God requires that the same act which upholds the righteous should punish the wicked."[70]

The original context of the passage treats the downfall of the enemies of God and also hints of the salvation of God's people.[71] The context gives, in part, a prophetic word from Moses concerning the future of His people, but the exact time of fulfillment is unclear, since the prophetic word is stated more in terms of a general promise. However it is easy to see how this promise could be associated with "the day of the Lord." So it is with the Hebrew's use, for with this quotation, the author most certainly has in mind the eschatological judgment . . .[72]

In the Old Testament, the day of the Lord may be any day of judgment. It appears, however, that the writer to the Hebrews has the final Day of Judgment in view in his quotation of Deuteronomy 32:35-36. Surely the Song of Moses in Deuteronomy 32 is a prophetic word that looks into the distant future.

If this is indeed the case, two questions arise. First, what is the calamity to which Deuteronomy 32:35 refers? Second, what is the exact meaning of the words "their calamity is near"? Calamity will come for those spurning the covenant and for those alien to the covenant who stand in opposition to God.

Looking ahead from the time of Moses, we think of two prominent times of judgment. Nebuchadnezzar destroyed Jerusalem in 586 B.C. Titus and the Roman armies again destroyed Jerusalem in 70 A.D. It was 1400 years before Christ when Moses penned his song recorded in Deuteronomy 32. This was over 800 years before the fall of Jerusalem at the hand of the Babylonians. It was almost 1500 years until the destruction of Jerusalem under Titus. If these calamities are in view in Deuteronomy 32:35, which may well be the case, they

---

[69] Philip Edgecumbe Hughes, *A Commentary on the Epistle to the Hebrews* (Grand Rapids: Eerdmans, 1977), 425.

[70] Brooke Foss Wescott, *The Epistle to the Hebrews* (Grand Rapids: Eerdmans, 1965), 332.

[71] Again, the reference is to enemies within and without the visible body. See both Hughes and Wescott.

[72] Beale and Carson, 981.

are hardly "near" as we understand the term. What then do these words mean, "their calamity is near"?

Calvin comments as follows in his 186th sermon on Deuteronomy.

> Now to knit up the matter withal, he says, *That the day of destruction draws near, and that their times are coming in haste.* This serves still to touch those the better, which do easily bear with their own faults, and cast the time behind their backs, as they say. But God tells us suddenly before they think of it, yes and even when they warrant themselves peace and rest, their destruction shall come upon them, accordingly as the Scripture does oftentimes put us in mind thereof, and not without cause.[73]

Sinners bear with their faults and think nothing of it. They consider they are due peace and rest. "[T]heir destruction shall come upon them."[74] In other words, destruction is certain. Calvin adds the following.

> The first thing then which we have to remember upon this place, is that we must have an eye to God's wrath a far off as though it were near at hand. The second is that we must be of good comfort when God seems to be as it were asleep and lets the wicked alone, and touches them not so much as with his little finger, but seems even to favor them. Let us assure ourselves that their state is never the better for all that.[75]

And why are the wicked not better off when God allows them to follow their desires and live in the paths of wickedness? "[T]heir destruction shall come upon them."[76] Their destruction is certain. This seems to be the meaning of Deuteronomy 32:35, "The day of their calamity is at hand, and their doom comes swiftly."[77]

From the perspective of the this eschatological song of Moses, Revelation 1:1, 1:3, 22:6, and 22:10 are not necessarily time-texts as Kenneth Gentry indicates. If we are correct in this short analysis of Deuteronomy 32:35, if Calvin is correct in his view regarding this text, and if Revelation builds on the eschatology of the Old Testament including passages like Deuteronomy 32, then, the above mentioned texts from Revelation are not time-texts. They do not speak of events from a chronological perspective. Rather, they set forth the certainty of the events portrayed in Revelation. These texts do not militate against a Philosophy of History view of Revelation neither do they push us into the Preterist position.

---

[73] John Calvin, *Sermons on Deuteronomy* (Carlisle, PA: Banner of Truth, 1987), 1158. Rendered in modern English. Italics part of the text.

[74] *Ibid.*

[75] *Op. Cit.*

[76] *Ibid.*

[77] English Standard Version.

Works Cited

Bannerman, James. *The Church of Christ*, 2 Volumes. Carlisle, PA: Banner of Truth, 1960

Calvin, John. *Sermons on Deuteronomy*. Carlisle, PA: Banner of Truth, 1987.

_____. *The Gospel According to St. John, 1-10*. Translated by T. H. L. Parker. Grand Rapids: Eerdmans, 1959.

Charnock, Stephen. *The Existence and Attributes of God*. Minneapolis: Klock and Klock. 1977.

Commentary on the New Testament Use of the Old Testament. Edited by G.K. Beale and D.A. Carson. Grand Rapids: Baker, 2007.

Gentry, Kenneth. *He Shall Have Dominion*. Tyler, TX: Institute for Christian Economics, 1992.

Henry, Matthew. *Matthew Henry's Commentary on the Whole Bible, 6 Volumes.* Grand Rapids: Fleming H. Revell, 1985.

Hughes, Philip Edgecumbe. *A Commentary on the Epistle to the Hebrews*. Grand Rapids: Eerdmans, 1977.

Kuiper, R. B. *The Glorious Body of Christ*. Grand Rapids: Eerdmans, 1958.

Murray, John. *Collected Writings of John Murray*, 4 vols. Carlisle, PA: Banner of Truth Trust, 1976-82.

Pieters, Albertus. *The Lamb, The Woman and the Dragon*. Grand Rapids: Zondervan, 1937.

Ramsey, James B. *The Book of Revelation: An Exposition of the First Eleven Chapters*. Carlisle, PA: Banner of Truth Trust, 1977.

Reid, William J. *Lectures on the Revelation*. Pittsburgh: Stevenson, Foster, 1878.

Ridderbos, J. *Deuteronomy*. Grand Rapids: Zondervan, 1984.

Rushdoony, Rousas John. *Thy Kingdom Come*. Nutley, NJ: Presbyterian and
    Reformed, 1970.

Swete, Henry B. *Commentary on Revelation*. Grand Rapids: Kregel, 1977.

Terry, Milton S. *Biblical Apocalyptics*. Grand Rapids: Baker, 1988.

Turretin, Francis, *Institutes of Elenctic Theology*, Translated by George
    Musgrave Giger. Edited by James T. Dennison. 3 Volumes. Phillipsburgh,
    NJ: Presbyterian and Reformed, 1992.

Wescott, Brooke Foss. *The Epistle to the Hebrews*. Grand Rapids: Eerdmans,
    1965.

Wilson, Geoffrey B. *Revelation*. Welwyn, England: Evangelical Press, 1985.

Worship in the Presence of God, Edited by Frank J. Smith and David
    Lachman. Greenville, SC: Greenville Seminary Press, 1992.

Scripture Index

184

185

Subject Index